"I cannot think of a better presentation of Francis, his life, and most particularly his vision than this splendid book."
Cistercian Studies Quarterly

"Jon Sweeney is good at many things, but he is a master at retrieving the treasure of the Christian past and restoring it to currency for the Christian present. In this book, he transcends even those categories. Francis of Assisi, a saint for every age, springs to life under Sweeney's attentive care."
Barbara Brown Taylor
Author of *An Altar in the World*

"Reflecting with Jon Sweeney on the work and wisdom of St. Francis of Assisi orients us on how to pray for Pope Francis's efforts and to respond to his initiatives."
Bert Ghezzi
Author of *The Heart of Catholicism*

"Jon Sweeney applies popular history to a man who changed history, St. Francis of Assisi. Deeply familiar with the Franciscan sources and writing in a very accessible style, Sweeney points to Pope Francis's inspiration. I like this book!"
John Feister
Editor-in-Chief of *St. Anthony Messenger*

"Sweeney writes very well and recreates critical scenes with admirable clarity."
Eugene C. Kennedy
America magazine

"This Francis is a Francis that readers may feel they are meeting anew and finding even more relevant in their lives."
Murray Bodo, O.F.M.
Author of *The Way of St. Francis*

Kintore College
75 Charles St W
Toronto, ON
Canada
416-944-8323

ALSO BY JON M. SWEENEY

Inventing Hell: Dante, the Bible, and Eternal Torment

Francis of Assisi: The Essential Writings (editor)

The Pope Who Quit: A True Medieval Tale of Mystery, Death, and Salvation

Mixed-Up Love: Relationships, Family, and Religious Identity in the 21st Century (with Rabbi Michal Woll)

The Age of the Spirit: How the Ghost of an Ancient Controversy Is Shaping the Church (with Phyllis Tickle)

Verily, Verily: The KJV — 400 Years of Influence and Beauty

Ireland's Saint: The Essential Biography of St. Patrick (editor)

Cloister Talks: Learning from My Friends the Monks

Francis and Clare: A True Story

Almost Catholic

The St. Clare Prayer Book: Listening for God's Leading

The St. Francis Prayer Book: A Guide to Deepen Your Spiritual Life

The Road to Assisi: The Essential Biography of St. Francis (editor)

WHEN SAINT FRANCIS SAVED THE CHURCH

How a Converted Medieval Troubadour
Created a Spiritual Vision for the Ages

Kintore College
75 Charles St W
Toronto, ON
Canada
416-944-8323

Jon M. Sweeney

AVE MARIA PRESS · AVE · Notre Dame, Indiana

Founded in 1865, Ave Maria Press is a ministry of the United States Province of Holy Cross.

www.avemariapress.com

Hardcover: ISBN-13 978-1-59471-486-3

Paperback: ISBN-13 978-1-59471-646-1

E-book: ISBN-13 978-1-59471-487-0

Cover image © Alfredo Dagli Orti/The Art Archive at Art Resource, NY.

Cover and text design by Brian C. Conley.

Printed and bound in the United States of America.

Library of Congress Cataloging-in-Publication Data

     Sweeney, Jon M., 1967-
  When Saint Francis saved the church : how a converted medieval troubadour created a spiritual vision for the ages / Jon M. Sweeney.
     pages cm
  Includes bibliographical references.
  ISBN 978-1-59471-486-3 (hardcover) -- ISBN 978-1-59471-487-0 (ebook)
  1. Francis, of Assisi, Saint, 1182-1226. 2. Spirituality--Catholic Church. I. Title.
  BX4700.F6S935 2014
  271'.302--dc23
  [B]
                    2014012018

CONTENTS

CONTENTS

A BRIEF CHRONOLOGY

1181   Francesco di Bernardone is born; the baby is named Giovanni, or John. Upon his father Pietro's return from a business trip, the boy is renamed Francesco, or Francis.

1204   Francis returns to Assisi, deflated, after failure in a military expedition.

1205   Francis begins spending long periods of time alone in prayer and reflection; he starts to care for lepers and soon goes on pilgrimage to Rome where he begs with the poor before old St. Peter's. Back in Assisi, he hears God speaking to him in the dilapidated church of San Damiano. He begins to live in San Damiano, while repairing it.

1206   Francis renounces his father, and the claims his father has upon him, with flair before a crowd in Assisi.

1208   Bernard of Quintavalle and Peter Catani become the first two to join Francis in gospel poverty. God reveals the Christian life to Francis in the Gospels when a local priest opens his missal three times—to Mark 10:17–21, Luke 9:1–6, and Matthew 16:24–28.[1] Before the year is out, Francis and eleven others walk to Rome to ask Pope Innocent III to approve their spiritual movement.

1219   Francis travels to Egypt at the height of crusading fervor and visits with Sultan al-Kamil.

1220   Francis abdicates leadership of the Franciscans and begins to lament how the friars are straying from his original ideals.

1221   Peter Catani dies and Brother Elias is elected the second Franciscan minister-general.

1223   On Christmas Eve, Francis creates the first live Nativity scene in Greccio, an Italian hill town sixty miles south of Assisi.

1224   Francis experiences what is called the holy stigmata (the world's first) upon Mount La Verna.

1225   Francis composes his "Canticle of the Creatures," the first vernacular Italian poem, as he celebrates life and contemplates death.

1226   Francis dictates his spiritual "Testament," the only writing of his to contain autobiographical details. He dies on the night of October 3 at Portiuncula, the small church he loved in the valley below Assisi.

PART ONE

A NEW LOOK AT FRANCIS

CHAPTER 1

WHY THE PAST MATTERS

*Where we see how the past illuminates the
present and how the spirit of Francis still
invigorates the Church.*

"I don't read many books about history," a friend told me
recently over breakfast at our favorite local diner. He
was peppering his hard-boiled eggs as he said it, and the
look on his face added, *Give me something I can* use. *Not a
history book.*

He wasn't interested in reading about long-dead people,
historical movements, or bygone eras. He wasn't jazzed by
"pivotal moments" of the past. None of that seemed relevant
to my friend, no matter how sexy the marketing copy.

I had just finished answering the question that I am often asked: "What are you working on?" My friend was over-
stating his position, for sure—although he likes to mouth off
a bit, he also reads a lot. But his reaction made me quickly
rethink my answer and try again.

"It isn't a 'history book,'" I started, emphasizing the
phrase I knew he disliked. "It's a great story of a strange, violent, and uncertain time about eight centuries ago, and one
particularly fascinating character. I'm writing about how a

distinct way of belief, behavior, and being got started by the conversion of a singular man named Francis, and how his optimistic faith resonates with and even shapes what I hear people saying they want more of today. . . ."

He was still listening, so I continued. "Okay, so it *is* history. But it's also about how well-meaning Christians almost killed the faith eight hundred years ago."

"Is that right?" Now I really had his attention.

"Yeah. And Francis of Assisi saw it coming and turned everything around. In many ways, he was an extremely normal guy. I mean, he had father problems, woman problems, expectations-of-others problems, but one day he began to listen more carefully to what his heart told him despite and beyond those problems. And as he got better at listening to his heart he realized that he was hearing God there.

"This ordinary guy began hearing God talking. That made him think he might be crazy. Maybe he was. But it turned out to be a good kind of crazy."

"There are 'good' and 'bad' kinds of crazy?" my friend asked with a smile.

"History proves it out—yes." I smiled.

"Francis never stopped being an ordinary guy, even when unusual religious things were happening to him, like hearing God's 'voice.' He questioned what he was hearing; he questioned whether he might be a complete fraud. And long after he vowed to remain single, focusing on God instead of women, he wondered if it had all been a mistake; maybe he should have just gotten married and raised a family like everyone else. I like that about him—how he kept doubting. I can relate to that.

"But the majority of people who met him, and heard him talk about faith, and watched what he did with his life, judged him to be sincere and sincerely inspired. For twenty years, thousands of men and women wanted to drop everything and walk the same path he chose. Though they followed a similar calling, they didn't simply pick up and imitate everything Francis did—following him around like the nitwits in Monty Python's *Life of Brian*—mostly because Francis wouldn't let them. Instead, he showed them how to change their lives where they lived. He was only trying to do what he thought God wanted him to do and encouraging others to do the same. Soon he saw that these followers, in the ways they were tapping into his spiritual vision, were—I realize that it sounds grandiose—well on their way to saving the faith.

"So," I wrapped up, "that's what I'm writing about. I want to tell that story."

"Interesting," he said. "We could use some of that today. Actually . . . maybe we are sort of in the midst of some of that now, too?"

"Exactly."

The Past Lives on in the Present

Isn't that why we read and talk about history? Because we are drawn to good stories. And because we hope we might discover how to make our story better today.

Our lives, whether we realize it or not, are wrapped up in about a dozen good stories at any given time, with trajectories and plots much larger than ourselves. Some of them reach back thousands of years, maybe even to the beginning of time.

We talk about history because it can illuminate our present times. This is different from saying what many people believe: that what happened in the past will be repeated in the future, but with different personalities and dates. Harvard philosopher George Santayana implied such a cyclic theory of history when he famously said, "Those who cannot remember the past are condemned to repeat it." That was in 1905, and the line was quoted again and again in the 1940s and '50s after our grandparents watched the mistakes of the First World War bring about the Second. But if the saying were really true, if there were truly nothing new under the sun, we'd never witness singular, seemingly inexplicable, events. We'd have to conclude that singular people—such as Gandhi, Van Gogh, Joan of Arc, Galileo, or, yes, Francis of Assisi—fit a mold. It doesn't take a genius to see that neither proposition is right. A cyclical view of history is a pretext for interpreting the past to mean whatever one wants it to mean.

This book approaches the story of Francis through a different understanding of the past.

The past lives in us, whether we are conscious of it or not. The past never leaves us. We carry it around in our memories, in our knowledge, even in our bones. Have you ever hurt a finger or toe and then, weeks later, perhaps even years later, suddenly felt that pain once again in precisely the same place where it first occurred, even while sitting still? We carry the past with us just like that, whether we want to or not. It was the Mississippi novelist William Faulkner who said, "The past is never dead. It's not even past."[1] So we occasionally read or study historical narratives in order to gain insight into what already, in some small way, animates our lives. In the reading, thinking, and discussing we come to understand better what lies deep within us.

Some stories have the ability to illuminate the present more than others. Sometimes we can identify clear moments, people, or events that stand out from the rest. Every era is chock full of detail because life is always full and complicated—so when history seems boring it is not so much because we can't see the forest for the trees, but because we have trouble seeing the seed that generated the forest or the spark that brought the forest down.

History easily becomes clogged. Yet there are signal figures who are catalysts for rapid change. They are worth focusing on, not only because examining their lives closely helps us understand a previous era, but because understanding them can tell us something important about who we are today. Francis of Assisi was such a figure: extraordinary, seemingly unlike and inaccessible to us normal people. Yet studying his life offers us a way to understand ourselves and our place on this planet better. Francis originated a spirit that still animates us, nearly eight hundred years after his death.

SEEKING THE *WHY*

So what do we talk about when we talk about history? We talk about people, conflict, words, actions, consequential decisions, results, evil, goodness, wars, and "winners" and "losers." We find them all in the story of Francis. But if we left it at that, we might as well read a middle school textbook or Wikipedia page. *Good* history seeks deep causes. *Why* did he do it? Why did his actions, words, decisions, or indecision result in *that*?

When we look at the events of Francis's life, we can easily see what he did, but it's more difficult to explain why. Every person in human history has been possessed of passions, motives, irrationalities, and the like, and few have left sure clues for deciphering them. Francis certainly didn't. Nevertheless, I believe that we can know a good deal about Francis's *why*.

Francis occasionally reveals his motives in his writings, but we have very few letters and bits of personal correspondence from his own hand. What we do have is often didactic though sometimes personal and even intimate. Still, it's tempting to imagine what has been lost. No one would have thought twice about tossing a note from the crazy young man from Assisi, written in 1205, 1208, or 1209, straight into the fireplace. One prominent medievalist puts it best when he yearningly speculates about Francis's beautiful but rare poem-songs: "Had we conserved the others, some of which we know were in Latin and some in Italian, still others perhaps in French, we would have a more complete picture."[2] Nevertheless, we know a good amount through what we do have.

Francis was not one to quickly and freely reveal his feelings. In that regard he was in step with every other man and woman of his era. Writing itself was unusual, and confessional writing almost unheard of. For key events in his life, such as calming the wolf in Gubbio, hearing the voice of God at San Damiano, and creating the first live crèche in Greccio, most of what we have are stories told by others. Francis didn't jot down what happened or what he felt. Instead, we have accounts written by those who knew Francis well, but weren't necessarily there to experience these events firsthand. Some of the stories seem too good to be possible. Other times, they ring true. Beyond these bare sources, we are left to conjecture; ultimately historians must use their imaginations, which should be tutored by a close familiarity with the subject and the sources.

Like every human being, Francis was full of emotions, confidence and self-doubts, strengths and "hang-ups," as well as motivations both conscious and unconscious. When we tell his story, we wade into these deep waters and do our best to see clearly. As with most historical figures who lived before the fifteenth century, we have to navigate through the fully formed and refined personae left to us by the early, adoring "biographers." Our understanding of Francis is mediated and affected, for good or bad, by the viewpoint of those who first told his story. Therefore, this book would have no spirit—and really no body—without my forming some psychological hypotheses. Without attempting to understand Francis's desires and motivations, I would have no hope of making sense of his life.

It is easy to follow his steps to see what Francis did on his personal road of conversion. Like a writer of suspense thrillers, I could describe our main character only or primarily through his actions, but that wouldn't get us very far. What motivated him? Why did he do what he did? Why didn't he do what he didn't do? These are the important questions we also need to attempt to answer. Along the way, you will see how Francis's conversion led prophetically and organically to a conversion of the Christian faith itself.

A FRESH WIND BLOWING

It was once said about an obscure Victorian novelist that the opinions he expressed were so original that few of his contemporaries took them seriously.[3] That almost sounds absurd, doesn't it? In our era, we've come to believe that original ideas bring recognition and success. Think Steve Jobs or Bill Gates. But those are only the ideas that we've been able to recognize, grasp, and implement, or the ones that create marketable commodities. Francis's ideas captivated thousands of people, in fact, hundreds of thousands across Europe and in the Middle East by the end of the first decade of his spiritual revolution. But, like the original ideas of that Victorian novelist, it would be easy to conclude that Francis's weren't taken very seriously. One gets the feeling from studying the life of Francis that, other than a few close friends, his contemporaries ultimately thought of him as a rather extraordinary idealist. Francis felt that there were few who really understood him, or were willing to follow, his lead to the letter.

Finally, before we begin to explore Francis's big ideas, let's pause to consider that his spiritual vision from eight centuries ago is already familiar to anyone paying attention to Pope Francis and the changing atmosphere in the Catholic Church today. Since he was elected in March 2013, there has been fresh air blowing into old and staid ways of doing things. Addressing the cardinals who elected him, Pope Francis said: "[O]ur life is a journey, and when we stop moving, things go wrong."[4] Isn't the Church supposed to be mainly about protecting what's forever good and true? Not so, said the Pope on the first day of his papacy. If we forget the past, take our eyes off the horizon, or if we value institutions over seeking the real goals of the Christian life, "things go wrong."

Something is happening. Is it too bold to suggest that another Francis may just be saving the Church again in the twenty-first century? There is plenty of idealistic hope in the air just now. After the Pope's trip to Rio de Janeiro in July 2013, one reporter put it this way: "Pope Francis is rescuing the faith from those who hunker down in gilded cathedrals and wield doctrine like a sword. The edifice of fortress Catholicism . . . is starting to crumble."[5] Many of us are watching carefully, and participating willingly, as that edifice softens into something less predictable, more godly. If something monumental happened eight hundred years ago to revive the Church, then it can happen again today; and the spirit that animated the earlier conversion may be quite similar to the spirit at work in the Church today. Much depends on what we ourselves will do.

CHAPTER 2

NOW, FORGET WHAT YOU'VE BEEN TOLD

Where we learn that the pious stories about Francis are misleading and begin to understand him as a man ahead of his time.

To prepare to meet the real Francis of Assisi, you will have to wipe clean the slate of your cultural and religious imagination and forget those half-formed legends. We all need to simply start over. As G. K. Chesterton said, "Truth, of course, must of necessity be stranger than fiction, for we have made fiction to suit ourselves."[1] I can promise that the Francis you will meet in this book is not the saint that you thought you knew, because that Francis is one of the most famous fictional characters of all time.

FRANCIS WAS NOT A STATUE

If you grew up going to Sunday school, try to forget what you saw and learned there about Francis: saccharine pictures and stories that keep us from seeing the real man. Further hindering our search for the truth is the fact that we often *prefer* those too-sweet images of Francis; they are comforting. Who doesn't want to sit on a quiet garden bench among blooming flowers, grasshoppers in song, and birds hopping about, with an image of Francis nearby? He is so serene and calming—especially when he's a cement statue.

Saints are always easier to handle than human beings. They do exactly what we expect of them, while humans rarely do. That is why Dorothy Day once famously said that she never wanted to be made a saint because it would be an easy way to dismiss her.

The saintly image of Francis is one that we can easily imagine inviting to tea. The cement Francis would stand quietly in the corner of the solarium among the ferns. He might tuck his napkin in his lap and mention the lovely songs the birds are singing just outside. Perhaps he would even interpret their songs for us, since he seems to be able to speak their language.

If you invited the real Francis to tea, he would likely insist on first standing out by the road to beg for his biscuits from passers-by, before joining you inside. His clothes would be ragged and dirty since he had little concern for presentation. Your neighbors would stare. They'd think you were hanging out with bums or inviting lunatics for a visit.

When people tell me they don't believe in God, I usually ask, "What God don't you believe in?" They invariably go on to describe a God who is judgmental, vengeful, overbearing, unloving, or whimsical. "Oh, I don't believe in that God either," I say. In a similar way, I have little interest in the cement Francis. Perhaps you feel the same way. I don't believe he ever existed. The real Francis wasn't known to sit in gardens with birds perched on his fingertips. However, he was the first Christian who seemed to understand how intimately human beings are connected to all other creatures. We diminish that profound insight when we distill it down to one sweet story and one freeze-frame fake image.

We need a new vision. We shouldn't be satisfied to see a fake or phantom of what is not really there. That would be like what happened in 1911 when the Czech writer Franz Kafka traveled from Prague to Paris in order to visit the Louvre. He queued up to visit not Leonardo's *Mona Lisa*, but the blank space on the wall where it usually hung, for it had been stolen a week earlier! Kafka (like thousands of others that year) went to the Louvre to see the legacy of the painting, not the real thing. Let's not go to see the legacy anymore. Let's look for the real person.

But our imaginations are limited by the baggage of previous experiences; knowledge can be conditioned by where we've been and what we've seen and heard. For many people, what they've seen and heard about the world's most popular saint has little to do with who he really was. It may be that the more learning you have, the less able you are to see the real Francis with fresh eyes. For this reason, I envy the person who comes to this book without any background in Sunday school or Catholic school, and without having read previous books about his legends and piety. You are able to take up *this book* and read without much prejudice, looking at Francis's life and spirituality with fresh eyes.

For those readers who know a great deal about Francis, I hope to offer a little deconstruction, transforming your image of Francis from readily familiar to freshly surprising. The real Francis is far more compelling and important than the imaginary one.

The very word *saint* contributes to our misunderstanding of Francis. Although I have great appreciation for the saints (have written books devoted to them, in fact), it is almost a shame that we use the word as often as we do. Many people hear *saint* and think *piety*, and unfortunately *piety* equals a sort of otherworldly irrelevance in people's minds. Also, some saints in history, particularly those that came after Francis's time, set out deliberately to become saints, almost the way a child today might grow up intent on becoming a doctor. Not that it is an unworthy goal—your mother and mine would probably approve—but this sort of spiritual self-consciousness is not at all characteristic of Francis. There's no evidence that he ever worried about his self-image or pondered crafting for himself the religious persona of a major figure in the Church.

I'm thinking now of saints like Angela of Foligno, Catherine of Siena, and Thérèse of Lisieux, of the late thirteenth, fourteenth, and late nineteenth centuries, respectively. Like Francis, each grew up in a small town (for Angela and Catherine, they were Italian towns quite near Assisi); but unlike Francis, each grew up self-consciously desiring to be recognized a saint in the eyes of God and the Church. When reading their writings, I find it difficult at times not to imagine a child looking into a mirror and wishing for something grand. You can imagine them earnestly looking at paintings of previous saints (primarily Francis), wanting to imitate the looks on their faces and the gestures of their hands. Where Francis self-consciously modeled his actions after the Jesus he met in the Gospels, many later saints read accounts of earlier saints like Francis in order to chart their paths and make their decisions according to what the blessed are supposed to do.

A line in Woody Allen's 1979 movie, *Manhattan*, comes to mind:

> "You think you're God!"
> "I . . . I gotta model myself after someone!"

It wasn't quite like that for Francis, because he moved toward the religious life very quietly and unassumingly. Besides, Francis's skills wouldn't have supported following a program for sainthood. He was never much of a daily planner. He wasn't much of a reader. He didn't even seem to stand still very much, except when he was alone and tired or in prayer. Ultimately, though, there simply were few public images of saints before the time of Francis. His life, in fact, marked a turning point in the "saints industry." He became the primary model for sainthood, although for him it was simply his path of conversion.

The real Francis was an unpredictable puzzle. His life was so full of stumbles and fits and starts that one could never accuse him of strategizing. We have trouble wrapping our minds around who he really was because he was so different from most everyone else. And he inadvertently transformed the whole notion of sanctity.

A New Approach to Francis

Francis is the world's most popular saint, as well as the primary inspiration for our new pope; but Francis of Assisi is misunderstood. More books have been written about him than about any other person in history but Christ, but much of what's been said and written is misleading or downright incorrect. Peter Barnes, one of the great playwrights of the late twentieth century, once said: "If you didn't know me you'd think I was a stranger."[2] Francis of Assisi might say that to us.

To set the record straight, this book takes a different approach from what you might expect in a book about Francis. You won't find many retellings of the famous legends here. This isn't comfort food—you can find that anywhere. Instead, I want to shine a light on six areas where Francis's life and message most transformed the Christian message and resurrected the original spirit of Christianity. That said, let me clarify that this book isn't only for people of faith. The Spirit of God inspires and challenges all people, and Francis and his spiritual vision are for everyone.

You will find chapters that build, one upon the next, looking closely at Francis's revolutionary approach to

- *Friendship.* There were clear and distinct lines of gender, religion, and status in his culture and time, and Francis crossed them all. Had he not also been of unimpeachable motives and character, he would have been burned at the stake for it.
- *The Other.* Francis demonstrated a profound respect for invisible, discarded, and demonized people, creatures, and other unknowns. He had nothing to gain by doing so, but he included them as equals in his life. This inclusiveness was the essence of how he changed monasticism and how he believed every person should act in the world.
- *Poverty.* Francis took poverty on personally and voluntarily, within and for himself, rather than simply as a subject of concern in the lives of others. He did not make poverty a virtue in and of itself, but he focused attention on how being poor was a sure way to understand the message of Jesus.
- *Spirituality.* Valued higher by Francis than theological understanding, his personal spiritual life set him apart from nearly every other leader in the Church in his day. If that sounds surprising then wait until you discover what the early thirteenth century was really like in the Western Church.
- *Care.* Francis was almost Buddhist in his gentle attention to, not just people and creatures, but things. It was his care-full-ness in little things that made him the environmental saint we

know today. In no other area do we see so clearly how Francis was a man ahead of his time.

- **Death.** Francis embraced death, not as a fatalistic gift, as did the majority of medieval people who talked in macabre ways about life as a "dance with death," but as an important part of living. His welcoming of death was almost without precedent in Christian teaching.

In each area, Francis forged a new spiritual path, anticipating the concerns of Christians (and people of every faith or none) right down to the twenty-first century.

A MAN AHEAD OF HIS TIME

Many interpreters of Francis's life have concluded that he was quite lonely in his mature years.[3] Why? Because he was so ahead of his time that very few people ultimately understood him. He started out by startling those closest to him with his fervor for personal faith, and then he had trouble finding anyone else who shared his vision—creatively, spiritually, emotionally. Like others in history who have led by example—doing, thinking, and talking about things that are beyond the lived experience of their contemporaries—Francis tended to be solitary when he wasn't leading. We see him again and again walking alone in the woods, off in a corner to pray by himself deep into the night, and striking out on some new course accompanied by a friar or two who didn't quite comprehend him. This wouldn't have been his first choice of how to live; he was actually a "people person." Add to this disconnect the fact that Francis lived according to nearly impossible ideals and you begin to understand why it is that thousands of people started down the path he began eight hundred years ago, but few were able to persevere. In the final half dozen years of his life, Francis felt that he had few true followers and even fewer friends.

A New Approach to Faith

In the chapters that follow you will notice several important things about Francis's spirituality that show him to be a man ahead of his time—perhaps a man for our time. For example, it will become clear that Francis was relatively uninterested in theological debates and creedal statements. When he states a belief in his writings it is most often regarding how one is supposed to behave toward others and the created world, not a matter of pure doctrine. Also, Francis was a man of deep faith who was agnostic on many of the details.

This is how a growing majority of Christians approach their faith today, so Francis might well fit in at most of today's churches in ways that he wouldn't have, say, 150 years ago. The minority view of a few centuries ago is now the majority perspective. We are more content today to leave some of the theological details behind, to remain agnostic, even, about them. Faith today is readily seen as concerned with many things other than what you believe—it includes hope, passion, family, love, story, virtue, commitment, and identity, all of which may seem more important than matters of creed.

Francis was also interested in finding faith beyond the walls of a church, unlike most people of his era. Faith in the thirteenth century was practiced almost entirely under the roof of a parish church, at those moments when one was partaking of the seven sacraments that defined a life with God. Church, font, altar, and priest were always necessary for finding God. So it is shocking that Francis talks little about the sacramental life. He always shows respect to priests, even though he chose not to be one, and he urges his brothers not to neglect Communion. But he often chooses to and encourages others to celebrate faith through beauty, song, and play, finding God in the woods, in others, or in art.

Francis of course lived in the pre-modern era. We live in the postmodern era. The two are often similar, which is another reason why Francis feels like a man for our time. Actively religious people of the thirteenth century were no more likely to define themselves by beliefs over practice than are active religious people today. The strikingly different era would be the sixteenth through the twentieth centuries, in which creed and dogma were king for most Christians. But for both the late medieval and the twenty-first-century faithful, doubt is an acknowledged companion to faith, rather than its enemy. We readily admit, without compromising our faith, that belief comes and goes; it is sometimes dark and uncertain and at other times can seem as strong as a bullhorn. If you feel that this is an accurate description of your faith, you're in great company, for Francis took a similar view.

One way to express Francis's approach is to say that his life was focused on *orthopraxy* (right action) over *orthodoxy* (right belief). Francis watched his contemporaries in religious life, the Dominicans, focus their ministry on teaching right belief, and in stark contrast he focused entirely on right action. The Gospel was not something to believe as much as it was a vocation to a changed life. When he preached, Francis tended to tell people the good news of God's love and desire to understand them, rather than preach what they should believe, or tell them they'd better go to Mass.

It is also instructive to pause and consider what Francis did *not* speak about. Nowhere in his writings does he mention his mother, for instance. Only indirectly does he ever speak of his father, as when he calls himself "the son of Bernardone," essentially an accusation of his own haughtiness. Bernardone was his father's patronymic and the name was given to Francis as a source of pride. He was—at least at some level—a disrespectful son; he believed that he couldn't ultimately respect his earthly and heavenly fathers, both.

A Converted Life
of Personal Poverty

Continuing to startle his followers and the Church, Francis didn't disdain the world, as medieval saints and ascetics were "supposed" to do. It is true that he occasionally used language to show a general disdain for his body, and he didn't treat himself kindly (something he later repented), but he also possessed a fully embodied approach to spiritual life, which we will see in some detail in the chapter on death. Francis's embrace of created things surprised people, even shocked and disappointed them. While turning away from the dominant world of power, money, selfishness, and individualism, Francis looked for eternal life in their opposites.[4] This included finding God's blessings all around him in the Creation and in other people, and in living a life of personal conversion—which means increasingly discovering who God intended him to be.

He was born with great privileges, so he knew what he was doing when he decided to forgo the power, comfort, and family money that came easily in his own life. Consider for a moment how odd this must have seemed to his friends and the friends of his father. What a disrespectful son he was for turning away from what his father had provided for him! In their more righteous moments, they probably told him that these things he disdained were actually God's gifts and graces to him. In a time when the disparity was huge between those who had and those who had not, why wouldn't Francis look upon "having" as a gift—even a divine gift? To do so would have made great sense.

Instead he decided to essentially "give back," even spurn, five bits of divine providence: comfort, convenience, material goods and benefits, position, and security. Why not simply thank God for them? Somehow they didn't communicate God to him. They didn't make godliness plausible in his life.

When Francis decided to turn his back on those privileges in order to turn toward God, he could have followed what others from his class and status had done by heading to the cloister. That would have been trading one sort of status and security for another that is more "spiritual." His father and mother, extended family, and friends, might not have liked that decision either, but there would have been some precedent for it.

A monastic vocation was often a good answer to one's unresolved childhood questions (and even neuroses). The Rule of St. Benedict goes to great lengths to lay out clearly which human problems do and which don't find solutions behind monastery walls. The rigors of monastic training, intended to begin in boyhood, were meant to provide physical safety, academic training, stability, and order to a young life.

But Francis wasn't drawn to monastic life. He came upon the scene at a time that was, in some respects, ripe for change. "The more youthful our age is, the more clear-sighted it will be," wrote one late-thirteenth-century lawyer.[5] Francis wanted a new kind of spiritual life that was somewhat unpredictable and without guarantees, putting him in less contact with religion and more contact with the living God.

A MOMENT IN TIME

In the mid-twentieth century, it was common for historians to make it seem that the world turned like a hinge on the moment, movement, or year that was the subject of their book. Let us take, for example, Martin Luther's nailing of the *Ninety-Five Theses* upon the door of the Castle Church in Wittenberg on October 31, 1517. Before this event, the summary reads, we have a corrupt Catholicism; after it, a tumultuous and reforming Protestantism. Wrong. History is always more complex than that.

But in recent years the pendulum has often swung too far in the other direction. We've sometimes democratized history to the extent that every historical moment comes out looking the same. Since we regard every era and year as important, we've come to think that the telling of history can be arbitrary, subject to the opinions and whimsy of the author. The narrator in Graham Greene's *The End of the Affair* memorably puts it this way in the novel's opening sentence: "A story has no beginning or end; arbitrarily one chooses that moment of experience from which to look back or from which to look ahead."

We know this is also wrong. Certain years really do matter more than others; stories have a real trajectory anchored in time. In the fourteen years between 1206 and 1220, for example, the foolish wisdom of a converted troubadour changed the world. So if you ask me what 1205 looked like in one of the hill towns or new cities within five hundred miles of the Mediterranean Sea, I will tell you a story of "Before." Ask me about 1221 (or perhaps 1226, the year Francis died) and I will tell you a very different story: the story of "After."

STYLE AS SUBSTANCE

Finally, if you have read anything before about Francis of Assisi, you may know that he admired the troubadour poets. These late medieval, mostly French entertainers at court first emerged early in the century of Francis's birth. They exalted romantic love to great heights; they personified love, comparing it to a knight, a crusader, a treasure-seeker; and they wrote of chivalry and fidelity in verse that was often put to song. The subtitle to this book refers to Francis as a "converted troubadour." You don't have to study the troubadours in order to understand Francis. I've done that for you.

The people who observed Francis in the earliest days of his spiritual movement witnessed him and his merry band of men acting, at times, like "God's jugglers." Francis himself called them *"jongleurs de Dieu." Jongleur* is a medieval French word meaning a wandering minstrel, a public entertainer, a professional storyteller. A *jongleur* was a troubadour—which also sometimes meant that he was an acrobat, fiddler, dancer, and poet. Troubadours were soulful in ways that made others want to hear and be entertained by them. By identifying himself as one of God's jugglers, Francis claimed who he wanted to be, and it looked very little like the role of a priest.

A man who often preached, Francis rarely ever preached in a church. He and his brother friars inspired and entertained more than they instructed. "God's jugglers" would express a personal, emotional faith with joy and song that reminded the people of the troubadours they'd heard in the public square, as well as ancient Italian folk traditions of song, dance, and carnival. The earliest Franciscans were interested in passion, fervor, and ecstasy—an intimate approach to God that was both playful and unpredictable.

Francis's father, the cloth merchant of Assisi, often traveled to and from France for his work. It was Pietro di Bernardone's love for all things French, in fact, that led him to name his son "Francis," which was not a common name for a boy on the other side of the Alps. One legend even has it that Francis's mother, Pica, of whom we know nothing for certain, was a Frenchwoman, married to Pietro on one of his business trips. It is safe to assume that their son, Francis, would have occasionally traveled with his father, picking up not only the language but French culture and style, as well. Even back home, humble troubadours were paid to sing, versify, and entertain in the courts of Italy beginning just a few years before Francis's birth.[6] But they were common in the places of travel known to his father for a half century before that. So when Francis called himself a troubadour, he had a profound knowledge of the role and presentation.

Francis was one of the first to establish a *jongleur* "school" in Italy—that's essentially what he and his friars were doing. He was writing songs and teaching his brothers to sing them in true troubadour style decades before the experts have identified the first Italian troubadour poet. It is astonishing to me that twenty-first-century professors of medieval poetry, and of the troubadours in particular, fail to acknowledge this fact. In an essay from the standard work on the subject used in university courses today, one scholar writes: "Troubadour imitation in Italian poetry begins with the formation of a 'Sicilian school' of poets, closely associated with the

Curia of Frederick II, between about 1230 and 1250."[7] Yet
that can't possibly be true, since Francis was imitating the
troubadours for at least two decades before that.

The point is, with a style and a spirit that rocked the
Church of his day, Francis changed the world. He effectively
"rebranded" the Church, if you will, with what he said and
didn't say, with what he emphasized and didn't emphasize,
and in the playful, powerful, unusual ways that he commu-
nicated the gospel message. It reminds me again of what's
happening in today's Catholic Church. Rediscovering some
of that early Franciscan charism, Pope Francis is communicating to the world that the style of the Church is changing,
even if the substance is not.[8] Pope Francis's first encyclical,
for instance, was devoted to the subject of joy—not to family planning or theology! With dramatic gestures, he has
changed the story of what the Church is about—by tapping
into a story that began about eight hundred years ago.

PART TWO

SIX WAYS FRANCIS QUIETLY CREATED A SPIRITUAL VISION FOR THE AGES

CHAPTER 3

THROUGH A HIGH VIEW OF FRIENDSHIP

*Where we observe Francis learning to
see the holiness in every person, making
friends at a leper asylum as readily as he
befriends the priests in town.*

F riendship had a primacy for Francis of Assisi. If you think of the traditional qualities of a saint, they're usually courage, intellect, and compassion. Francis had these virtues, some of them in spades, but for him the list simply started elsewhere. Francis's journey began and ended with—and his charism comprised almost entirely—a true and unique gift for *friendship*.

This is a man who was a living saint in the eyes of those who knew him, and yet he never ceased to be a real mensch, an ordinary good guy if you will. He began his religious life looking to the Gospels in order to imitate the life and follow the expectations of Jesus, and through that endeavor he discovered how to be a friend first and foremost. As Chesterton once said, "The Christian ideal has not been tried and found wanting; it has been found difficult and left untried."[1]

Francis developed a simple kindness, openness, and neighborliness that is part and parcel of gospel living. Always looking out for the needs of others, he responded to each person he met as if he were already a friend. And yet Francis also knew how to develop close relationships with a certain few; throughout his life we see him leaning on friends like Brother Leo and Sister Clare. We may think of saints as aloof or mostly alone with God, but not this one. He became a saint through friendship.

He loved his closest friends so much that he even knew how to make light of himself, giving himself a nickname when talking with his brothers. In a letter to Brother Leo he wrote, "Peace and good health from your Brother Francis-Sco!"[2] We don't expect that sort of playfulness in a saint! This was a simple man whose primary expressions of faith were profoundly human. There needn't be anything spiritual about being a good friend, but Francis made it into a holy art form.

BACK TO THE BEGINNING

Francis's conversion took a long time. You might say that it took his entire life; perhaps all of ours do. When you look closely, you can see that Francis's conversion sparked from kindling to fire when he became confident enough in himself to discover real friendship.

Before that happened, Francis was friendly with everyone. As a teenager, he seems to have embraced nearly every person he knew, probably because he wanted so desperately to be liked. He was probably fun to be around—the evidence suggests it. I think of Francis as a boy working in his father's shop when I hear this children's nursery rhyme that may have medieval origins: "Girls and boys, come out to play, the moon doth shine as bright as day. Leave your supper, and leave your sleep, and come with your playfellows into the street. Come with a whoop, come with a call, come with a good will or not at all. Up the ladder and down the wall, a halfpenny roll will serve us all." He was a playful child, then a playful teenager.

There's no harm in that sort of life—except if you grow up and don't learn that there's more. A child-turned-adult might think that play is all that friends do, but of course it isn't. So Francis was friendly with all, but really friends with none. He derived his identity from his companions. He was the life of the party and always had people around, but it left him feeling profoundly empty.

Francis resembled the young Augustine, who thus described himself at the age of eighteen in his *Confessions*: "I came to Carthage, and all around me in my ears were the sizzling and frying of unholy loves. I was not yet in love, but I loved the idea of love."[3] Francis, too, was full of the feelings of love at age eighteen, inspired by the poets whom he read and reread, long before he knew what love meant. Like many a young man, he felt the stirring of romantic emotions move his soul. At that age, romantic love can feel downright religious in the urgency of the response it demands. Francis danced and sang, so full of joy when he thought of the face of his beloved and the touch of her lips on his own. He became an evangelist for love, telling anyone who would listen that he was blessed with profound emotions.

A Failed Adventure
Brings Change

In 1204, at the age of twenty-three, Francis was still his father's son, unconsciously pursuing what his father valued: reputation, status, and wealth. He possessed a desire for adventure, too, being a young man raised on storybooks of knights and treasures. So he saddled up in fine armor purchased by his dad and headed out to war in a local skirmish between Assisi and a neighboring town; that is what young men from Assisi did if they wanted to earn the respect of their elders. Leaving behind the young women whom he loved made this new journey all the more poignant and romantic.

Francis felt very grand and grown up, but he wouldn't have made an impressive figure in the saddle. He wasn't erect and confident, and he wasn't a horseman. It turned out that his armor was readier for battle than he was, and he soon returned home, slightly wounded or humiliated, possibly both. The tradition says that he may have even deserted.

There is an intimate connection between self-image, humiliation, and true spiritual conversion. We occasionally need humiliation in order to see ourselves correctly. When Francis returned to the home of his parents, disgraced and humiliated, those whom he thought were his friends began to talk about him behind his back, to question his courage, his manhood. What else does a man have but his reputation? Francis began to question himself, feeling lost and uncertain.

He heard the murmuring around him, most of all from his father, Pietro, who wasn't subtle about his own displeasure. Pietro grumbled to friends about his son, and he would question him directly. *Won't you get up and do something?*

he probably said more than once, while Pica, his wife, took a more comforting approach. Meanwhile, Francis looked in the mirror in his parents' house and didn't like the person he saw.

You don't have to be a psychoanalyst (only read the biblical stories of Abraham, Isaac, and Jacob!) to know that we all need to shake off the effects of childhood in order to become our mature selves. It was then, still in 1204, that Francis began to change. A new vision of the possibilities of life opened inside of him. When his old friends came calling, he began to tell them that he was busy. With what, they wondered? He'd always been so available and now, surely, he needed them more than ever. Even according to *The Little Flowers of Saint Francis* (compiled by a friar a century and a half after Francis's death), in which the tales told of Francis sometimes maintain a too-rosy glow, Francis seems muddled in those early days of his conversion:

> It was in the days when Francis was still wearing his secular clothing, even though he had begun to renounce the things of the world. He had been going around Assisi looking mortified and unkempt, wearing his penance in his appearance in such a way that people thought he had become a fool. He was mocked and laughed at, and pelted with stones and mud by both those who knew him and those who did not. But Francis endured these things with patience and joy, as if he did not hear the taunts at all and had no means of responding to them.[4]

Francis had turned his attention away from his former pastimes. He was often alone with God, praying and contemplating, which was all new to him. Over the next year,

Francis began to develop his first real friendship—with God—and it came through time spent alone together. He listened carefully to God speaking in his heart and soul, as well as in the world around him, and he began to uncover a kind of friendship that he'd never known before. This new sort of relationship was based not on parental expectations, gender roles, or societal norms—the ways of the *old* troubadour—but on coming to know who he was and what God desired from him. The self-understanding he gained from learning to be quiet and listen made Francis's conversion possible. He had to learn to be quiet in order to hear the Divine, who usually speaks softly. And it was God's friendship with Francis that taught him how to be a true friend.

As Henri Nouwen wisely wrote, "First, silence makes us pilgrims. Secondly, silence guards the fire within. Thirdly, silence teaches us to speak."[5] And soon Francis was ready to turn back toward others with open arms; he'd always been gregarious and outgoing, but now he carried a true love inside of him. He became fun-loving once again, only now the joy and adventuresome spirit of the old troubadour were in service to a higher purpose. The ecstatic feelings of love were back, too, but not only when a young woman he fancied was nearby. With the help of the Gospel, which he began to listen to carefully, Francis began to break down the barriers to friendship inherent in his old worldview. Every person, he began to see, was at the most basic root the same.

UNIVERSAL FRIENDSHIP

Francis gradually became someone who made it his adventure to find and befriend people in hiding, societal outcasts as he himself had recently been. Perhaps also these new friends were less likely to remember who he'd once been. Now, where he'd once serenaded ladies with poetry and song, Francis began to turn these arts toward an equally extravagant love for strangers.

The Spanish philosopher Miguel de Unamuno once suggested that astronomy and poetry are two fields of endeavor that owe their existence to idleness. In other words, sitting still and being attentive are necessary requirements for noticing that some stars are brighter than others and that some celestial bodies move. An occasional quick glance at the sky won't show those things to you. It is the same with poetry: only a sensitive soul with patience and time will be able to write it well. And so it is also with the art of friendship. Francis had taken the time to listen, look, and observe, and now he turned his passion toward others.

First, he joined in a pilgrimage to Rome, walking for weeks (much to the consternation, again, of his father) to the Holy City, seeking both answers to new spiritual questions and other people who were asking the same sorts of questions. In the square in front of St. Peter's Basilica, he joined the homeless poor in begging for his bread, as he now realized that Jesus had praised what was so commonly despised by the Christians he grew up with: namely, poverty and insecurity. Praise of poverty was something he'd never heard in church before, let alone at home. At the beginning of the Beatitudes we read, "Then [Jesus] looked up at his disciples and said: 'Blessed are you who are poor, for yours is the kingdom of God. Blessed are you who are hungry now, for you will be filled'" (Lk 6:20–21). Francis suddenly realized that the people his father had told him were unworthy of care and coin were in fact precious. And they were also his brothers.

Then his understanding of brotherhood continued to expand. Next, he befriended lepers. In the early thirteenth century in Italy, lepers were separated from communities, indeed from all healthy people. They were forced to live apart in lepers' hospitals, which were not really hospitals at all. We'd shudder to see the conditions there. So there is nothing unusual about the fact that Francis grew up loath to touch any leprous person. No sane person did. But he overcame this fear and decided to befriend even these outcasts, touching them and carrying water to wash their sores, all of which was actually forbidden by law. We have no evidence that he served from a sense of pity, feeling sorry for himself or the lepers, but only that he was being a friend. As Simone Weil wrote in *Gravity and Grace*, "Love is not consolation, it is light."

From that point on, Francis was always seeking out people in hiding, and he didn't care much what others thought about his new friendships. Francis's expressions of friendship came from his heart in an uncalculated way. We see Francis befriending without judging, noticing and responding to people's needs, and expressing love simply because that person has been created by a God who says that every created thing is good.

The Converted Troubadour

Francis's first biographer, Thomas of Celano, is almost poetic in his description of Francis early in his conversion, as he was beginning to throw off the things of the world associated with his rich father: "He who had previously enjoyed wearing scarlet robes now traveled around half-clothed."[6] This is where the hippie images of Francis originate. We can almost see him: dressing in rags, forgoing his father's fine silks, hanging out with the destitute, still strumming and singing drinking tunes of romantic love, but directing them now toward God rather than lovely women. Here was a new kind of troubadour—one for God.

There was a gulf between sacred and secular music in those days. Sacred music took as its subject the Bible and the liturgy; its composition and performance were restricted to those with a certain amount of education, and it was to be performed in a sacred setting. Secular music was for everyone else—the majority of people who never had opportunities for formal learning—and everywhere else.

We know that Francis had relatively little education; his parents may not have thought it necessary for a rich merchant's son, and it's easy to imagine Pietro believing that the travel abroad that young Francis had experienced was more than enough to educate his bright boy. So when Francis turned to making music, his music was of the secular, not the sacred, kind, and he performed it in a secular rather than sacred setting.

The next sentence in Thomas of Celano's narrative tells us of an occasion in a forest when "Francis was singing praises to the Lord in French and thieves surprised and attacked him." These wandering ruffians were surely disappointed to find nothing of value on their hapless prey. "Who are you?" they demanded. "The herald of the great King! What's it to you?" Francis rejoined, speaking imprudently like the young man he still was. So they beat him up and threw him in the snow. Then, Thomas says, "When they'd left, Francis rolled around in that snow with joy and once again began to sing in the woods, louder than before, with praise for God."[7]

A New Form of Religious Life

By this point he'd learned at least three things: how to be quiet and spend time alone, how to be with others in true friendship, and how all sorts of self-confidence and joy stems from an original friendship with God.

Then Francis had a friendship crisis. The more time he spent alone with God, the more time he wanted to do just that. But with only so much time in a day, he felt the pull of the active versus the contemplative life. Friendship with others and friendship with God came into conflict.

On the one hand, he'd learned to love to be alone with God and pray, and he would walk by himself into the Umbrian countryside and commune with his Creator, or sit alone in an abandoned church for hours and days. He loved those times when he was hidden from the world around him but completely exposed to the Divine.

On the other hand, Francis felt drawn to being with others—to working out his new faith in front of, and in friendship with, other people. He also listened to the Gospels carefully, noting that Jesus told his followers to help each other, to befriend each other, to eat with one another (even with one's enemies), and to walk through life in the company of other people. So Francis was in a quandary. Which way should he go? He couldn't fully devote himself to both ways of life.

The two existent modes of a religious life illustrated the possibilities. Francis knew of hermits: men who led isolated lives of prayer, removed from monasteries. And he knew how most monks lived, as part of a community that prayed, worked, lived, ate, and slept in close quarters with their fellow monks, although they too prayed often in private. So one day Francis asked two of his closest friends to guide him. How, he asked, does God want me to live? The answer from Sylvester and Clare came back unanimously: Francis was supposed to be a friend to others, first and foremost. He listened to their advice and decided that he would neither become a cloistered monk nor run off to his beloved Apennine Mountains to be a hermit.

There was clearly a touch of the genius about Francis, and we can thank his haphazard, wandering spiritual education for some of that. Just as we are grateful to Mozart's father for not keeping young Wolfgang stuck in a cathedral school in Salzburg practicing his piano, and we're grateful that Mohandas Gandhi didn't enter traditional provincial politics when he returned to India after his stay in South Africa, we can be thankful that Francis did not become a traditional monk or hermit. The walls of the cloister would have contained him, and the hermit's isolation would have kept him from exercising his gift of true friendship. Instead, he created a new way of life—the way of the friar.

A friar made vows like monks did, but these did not include a vow of stability. A friar was supposed to go wherever the Spirit or his fellow brothers told him to go, preaching and exhibiting the Gospel. This they did from the beginning, which is one of the primary reasons why the Roman Curia was never as excited about the spirituality of early Franciscans as were the people whom the Franciscans served. Friars were unpredictable. Much "safer" are religious orders where the monks stay inside and quietly pray. Multiply the ecclesiastical worries of the Curia when a woman joins Francis as the first female "brother" on Palm Sunday, 1212.

Francis and Clare,
Men and Women

The relationship between Francis and Clare has confused people for centuries. We have trouble imagining how a man and a woman who were as emotionally and spiritually close as the two of them were, couldn't have been something more than just friends. However, keep in mind that Francis was thirteen years older than Clare, which may not mean much when two people are forty-three and thirty, but means a great deal when they are, say, twenty-six and thirteen. Clare was only thirteen when Francis's conversion was in its early stages of fermentation.

Francis and Clare definitely shared important personal qualities, including courage. Francis showed courage in his twenties when he stood up to his father, who did all he could to thwart his son's plans to abandon a life of upper middle-class security for what must have seemed like spiritual bohemianism bordering on the certifiable. Bear in mind, Francis didn't come to his father one day and say, *I think I'd like to join a monastery*. Or, *Father, I would like to study to become a priest*. Instead, he read the Gospels, listened to the Spirit, and gradually, step by step, began to put Jesus' teachings into practice, regardless of how it looked to others. There's no question that, in the eyes of the people of Assisi, Pietro di Bernardone would have been the sane one, not his son Francesco.

A few years later, Clare showed her own mettle, standing up to her *famiglia* the way she did. Imagine it, for a moment: While still a teenager, Clare left her secure home full of kin and servants, spurning the promise of a safe and secure marriage, and walked across Assisi in the middle of the night to join Francis's group of men. There was some sort of understanding before she arrived that night, because Francis expected her coming. They both must have been frightened. What in the world would people think? A girl doesn't just leave her parents' home and move in with a bunch of guys! And a respectable man, let alone one who claims to be a religious leader, doesn't accept a girl, under such circumstances, into his group. Does he?

It is this dramatic situation, and maybe our own easy tendencies to see the sexual lurking behind every relationship, that has led a novelist to write of Francis and Clare as lovers and a filmmaker to make their love even more enticing by portraying it as both erotic and sexually unfulfilled.[8]

That night, when Clare arrived to join the growing band, Francis cut her hair. This procedure was (and is still) called a tonsure, and made Clare a "friar" like the others. Francis, in fact, called her one of his "brothers," not because he didn't realize that she was a young woman but because he had no other, better word for what her relationship with the other friars would be.

But there is a certain sadness to this part of the story because it was not long after Clare's nighttime flight to Portiuncula—a name that means "little portion," Francis's diminutive for the chapel that they called home—that she, together with a younger sister who soon joined her, were sent to live a cloistered life. Francis and Clare surely arrived at this decision jointly. They knew that the world wasn't ready for women and men to do God's work side by side, and they couldn't risk jeopardizing their work by upsetting too many cultural norms at once. The women went first to the convent of San Paolo de Bastia, a couple of miles away, and then, perhaps a week or two later, to the Benedictine convent of Sant'Angelo upon Mount Subasio.

Both Clare and Francis accepted that they couldn't try to live out this gospel experiment with the sexes together in the divine work. There is little evidence of how long the women and men of the early Franciscan movement worked side by side before the women were separated. For how many days were they all simply friars? That's surely what Francis wanted. It could have been only one or two days, perhaps a few, precious weeks.

Still, the friendship between Francis and Clare remained profound. We see him alternating between wanting to leave her alone, nun that she was (for what would people think?), and traveling to her for spiritual guidance. For her part, Clare wanted to be with Francis, her friend, and they both knew that Clare often had the perfect "word" for Francis's soul. He needed her. They needed each other. Throughout their lives together—because friends don't have to live nearby in order to be close—she was like a deep, still well to his full, fast-flowing river.[9]

EXPERIMENTS IN FRIENDSHIP

There is an ancient tale of a man who falls in a pit, which has been dug deep enough to keep a man from climbing out of it, along an old Roman road. Many people travel along the road, see the man down in the hole, and do nothing but look. Eventually, a monk comes along and stops to pray with the man, for it is noon—time for the Angelus, when everyone stops in thanks and prayer.

"Now will you help me out?" the unfortunate man asks the monk when the prayers are completed. "I don't have the strength," the monk tells him, and gives the man a blessing and walks on.

Next comes a healer. He sees the man in the hole and pauses long enough to offer some advice as to how the trapped man should care for his wounds. "Can you help me out, now?" the man in the pit asks him. "I'm unable," he is told, and the healer moves on.

Next come an orator and a lawyer. Together these two stand beside the hole and condemn whoever dug such a pit, surely the practice of slave traders. After convincing many who walk by that this practice must be punished more severely by the Roman Senate, they move on, leaving the man in the hole.

Finally, one of the unfortunate man's friends comes walking by. The man in the pit is elated until suddenly his friend jumps in right next to him. "What are you doing!" the unfortunate man screams, "Didn't you realize that I was stuck down here?" His friend replies, "Yes, but I wanted to see the pit from your perspective. Now, we'll figure a way out together."

This is how we see Francis living out friendship over the next twenty years. He treats friendship like a free gift that is his to give to anyone. He takes the Gospel as his sourcebook in order to understand both the obstacles and the solutions to life's problems, but he puts himself on the line in order to show others how and where to go. We see Francis sitting in boats with fishermen who are anxious about their small catches. He visits towns where rivalries are splitting people apart. He works side by side in the fields with people before he ever says a word about God to them. He wants to sit and talk with a sultan in order to understand him better.

Thomas of Celano refers to Francis repeatedly as "the holy man" and "the holy man of God" as he tells stories from his life, but the stories themselves don't reveal someone who thought of himself in those terms. "May the Lord give you peace," was Francis's most common remark to people. What a contrast this was to the apocalyptic fear-mongering of most other wandering spiritual groups in those days, and

how different it was even from the doctrinaire preaching of
the new Dominican Order.

Francis made friends deliberately and easily, seeking
people out and showing them, quite simply, that he cared for
them. This is not to say that he did not have close friendships
in the more traditional sense. He had close associates, men
and women who were his trusted companions and confi-
dantes, and who showed care and love for him in return. To
be a good neighbor and friend, he needed a support system,
beginning with his own religious family.

LIFE WITH THE FRIARS

But we don't see Francis standing outside or "above" his
brothers, even when he's exhorting them to do something. The early sources such as Thomas of Celano's first biography say that the friars "did not hide from him the least of
their thoughts or even immediate impulses of their souls."[10]
He usually talked about the spiritual life in ways that showed
he was no different from anyone else, such as in the "Letter
to All the Friars" of 1225 when he wrote, "Almighty, eternal,
just, and merciful God, give us scoundrels your grace to do
for you what we know you want from us and always to do
that which is pleasing to you."[11] Earlier in the same letter, he
prefaced one of his exhortations by saying, "With all the love
I am able to offer, kissing your very feet, I therefore beg you
. . . ," and one gets the easy feeling that he wasn't speaking
metaphorically.

The friars lived intimately, close together. These were not
monks with neat and secure cloister cells, walls on which
to hang their religious art, shelves for their personal books,
doors that closed. Imagine instead the makeshift abode of a

homeless man that you meet on a street corner and you'll be closer to what was true for the first Franciscans, except that they slept not on street corners, but usually in caves or fields. The structural impermanence of their way of life, however, must have both fostered and challenged friendship. Such friendship is not for everyone. Francis and his brothers lived so closely together that privacy was almost impossible. The native difficulties of their situation remind me of some of the remarks left behind in Dorothy Day's letters and diaries about the simultaneous blessedness and messiness of the early Catholic Worker houses. We know from non-Franciscan historians writing in the thirteenth century that thousands of people came to join Francis in the first decade of his religious life. Many stayed, but many couldn't take it and left.

In one of the most personal of all the writings of Francis we possess, this one from 1226, Francis writes a note of encouragement to his closest male friend, Leo, using a metaphor for his affection that is somewhat surprising:

> I am speaking to you, now, as a mother would, because all of the words we passed between us on the road together I am summarizing in this message and bit of advice. If you ever feel the need for my counsel, I suggest that you turn to this letter.
>
> My advice is this: In whatever way you feel called to serve the Lord, and to make him happy, to follow his footprint and his poverty, do that, and do that with my blessing and with the blessing of the Lord God.
>
> And if you ever want to come and see me, Leo, for the sake of your soul or for any other reason, come, by all means, come back to me.[12]

Francis often used familial terms to talk about his relationships with his spiritual brothers. They were to care for each other like mothers and sons, he said, taking turns being the "mother" or the "son" depending on one's needs in the moment. A son remembers his love for his mother differently from all other loves; it is more than simply affection; it is unconditional.

The metaphor would have been well known to Leo. Francis had memorably used it before in his "Rule for Hermitages," written nine years earlier to all the friars, for those times when they desired to spend extended times in seclusion for purposes of contemplative prayer:

> Any among us who desire to stay in religious hermitages should do so in numbers of three, or, at the most, four. Two of these brothers should be "the mother" and two—or at least one, "the sons." The two who are mothers should follow the life of Martha, and the sons should follow the life of Mary. . . . The brothers who are mothers should aim to stay far away from others and to protect their sons from all, so that they are never spoken to. And the brothers who are sons should not talk with anyone but their mothers. . . . Now, "sons" may occasionally take on the role of "mothers," as brothers take turns in these spiritual roles by mutual agreement.[13]

It was this egalitarian approach to friendship that led Francis to be acclaimed a saint long before his death, in the way that saints used to be "made"—by popular demand.

A GOOD HUMAN BEING

Francis's many experiments in friendship taught him to see the holiness in every person. He made friends at San Salvatore delle Pareti, the leper asylum below Assisi, just as readily as he came to know the priests in town. He cared for the lepers, following Christ's instructions to tend to the ailing as if they had the face of God, just as he wrote of his utmost respect for priests as ones who carefully handle the body of God. And these special friendships came to him as easily as those he formed with ordinary people around town. Following what he found revealed in the Gospels, Francis strove to be a good human being, not to become a saint.

Francis lived in an era that was, for all practical purposes, without atheists. Surely there were some who in their heart of hearts did not believe in the existence of a God, but they didn't and couldn't possibly say it out loud. They wouldn't even admit it to their spouses for fear of the Inquisition. In this somewhat artificial way, Christians in the Middle Ages were all the same. What would distinguish a Christian as unique in such an era was to embody the teachings of Jesus in daily life. And Francis did.

The Baal Shem Tov, the founder of the Hasidic movement of Judaism in eighteenth-century Poland, is perhaps someone we can compare to Francis on the art of friendship. The Baal Shem showed the same sort of impulsive, instinctual, joyful love for other human beings as Francis did. People were naturally drawn to the Baal Shem's spiritual priorities because they were drawn to the man who embodied them.

Another example might be Gandhi, who was so revered in twentieth-century India that he could influence the destiny of millions of people simply by refusing to eat until they heeded his advice, or did what he was urging. Gandhi held that sway because he loved and was loved like a friend. Francis never tried to wield that sort of power, but the comparison is apt; his influence came from his enormous popularity among everyday people, and that influence was built quite unconsciously one love at a time. And for both Gandhi and Francis, their influence waned immediately after they died, so dependent was it upon their personalities and the spirit of their personal friendships.

CHAPTER 4

BY EMBRACING THE OTHER

Where we learn that Francis saw a different world from the one perceived by most religious people of his time—he saw the "sacred" in everyone and everything.

Most famous figures in history, and particularly most saints, are distinguished by personal characteristics of unusual endurance (grit), strength (of mind and spirit), and certainty. Let me suggest that Francis is an exception to this generalization, and that he wouldn't be disappointed to hear me say it. He has a human, accessible quality that appeals to those who feel themselves outside of the norm, somewhat weak, or simply unsure.

Throughout his life we see Francis, again and again, especially at critical moments, and often just before he's about to do something that becomes iconic, doubting himself. He knew that he wasn't doing the religious life the way it is necessarily "supposed" to be done, and sometimes it worried him. Besides, aren't prophets supposed to walk and talk with assurance?

Early biographers relate stories of Francis going off to be alone and pray in secret. He often withdrew to interrogate himself, or to ask God, "Why?" We read of these moments secondhand, through the memories of brothers who surprised Francis while he was "in prayer," which seems to have been euphemistic for every occasion when he was alone. They often can't or don't hide the anxiety, spiritual and psychological, that they sense he's feeling. It is as if this internal struggle is essential to the man who was their friend. This quality of vulnerability reveals that Francis considered himself something of an "other" and is part of his down-to-earth appeal to ordinary people like us.

A New Method of Spreading Christian Influence

Henry David Thoreau once said, "What can be expressed in words can be expressed in life."[1] He might as well have been talking about Francis, who always chose to speak most clearly with his actions. In contrast, when you look at the lives of other medieval Christians who made an impact on the secular institutions and leaders of the world, you generally see two, more common, ways in which they did so.

First, there were those who claimed power and authority directly from God. Anyone walking around Rome today can see from the alternating statues and memorials that popes and Caesars were in close competition with one another two thousand years ago. Then, popes and Holy Roman emperors fought each other for power, sometimes even militarily. The clever popes (and cardinals, etc.) were the ones who claimed their power over and against the rulers of the state. Looking back through history, we see popes crowning emperors, bishops excommunicating princes, and secular rulers kow-towing to the demands of their religious leaders. These religious leaders usually declared that the state was subject to the Church by divine design. This is how most of the strong religious leaders attempted to rule their territories and people: by taking power from power.

There were also Christians who set out on a second path: they became politicians themselves. Think of the early crusading era and the figures of Bernard of Clairvaux and Peter the Hermit. These men knew how to influence kings and princes; they were smart about affecting public opinion, and then also about getting what they wanted or what they felt God and Church needed.

Native to both of these ways of exerting Christian influence in the world was the belief that the sacred and the secular were opposites, as well as opposed to each other.

Francis found a new, third way of influence because he viewed the world itself differently. He looked around and literally saw a different world from the one perceived by most popes, cardinals, bishops, priests, and monks. Everything in the world looked sacred to him. God's work (action, not words) was to be done no matter where one happened to be, and everywhere one happened to be possessed holy potential. So, whereas Bernard of Clairvaux may have done his politicking in imperial and papal courts and then returned to the cloister or the woods in order to find God in personal contemplation, Francis came along and found his godly work wherever he was—in the village, in the fields, in the midst of an argument between people, with Muslims or soldiers, or while walking with a companion along the seashore.

This third way is the key to understanding how Francis was able to see the "other" in his milieu. Simply put, for Francis there were no "others."

He didn't prioritize the powerful. In fact, he wrote a little-known "Letter to Those Who Rule over People" in which he went out of his way to remind "you who are mayors, councilmen, magistrates, and governors throughout the world . . . that our day of death is coming soon. I plead with you: do not ever forget the Lord our God." He went on to urge them to see the people whom they govern or rule as "people who are entrusted to your care," not mere subjects. And he asked every magistrate to periodically take time for receiving the Eucharist, and to remind the people in their care to do the same.

In his admonitions to his own order, Francis most often asked his brothers to be giving and open to others. Hospitality to all was the chief Franciscan virtue besides personal poverty. When you combine this with his radical way of including animals, plants, fish, insects, and even inanimate objects in his spiritual vision (more on that later), Francis took the teachings of Jesus about hospitality, in practice if not in theory, to an almost nondualist extent: his spiritual practice emphasized the ultimate, essential interconnectedness of all things. All creatures, certainly all people (even "bad" ones like thieves), and even many inanimate objects were treated as if they were part of the One.

LEARNING THROUGH LISTENING

One of the ways many have misunderstood Francis is in assuming he was an anti-intellectual. It may be technically true, but the term doesn't say all that needs to be said about the ways Francis learned. He lived in an era of widespread illiteracy when book learning was something enjoyed by the very few. Reading required time and money, and only the wealthy and cloistered religious had both.

"Anyone born a poet [during the Middle Ages] became an architect," Victor Hugo famously said in *The Hunchback of Notre-Dame*, by which he meant that most people desirous of learning were drawn to the inside of great churches.[2] There really were no books for everyday folk. We probably see more printed words in a week today than even a medieval scribe or scholar saw in a lifetime. Most people had to study the symbols and architecture of churches in order to learn.

But Francis wasn't one for book learning (hence the label), and he wasn't an architect. His only real interest in architecture was to rebuild old churches when they became too dilapidated to stand up anymore. Yet he was a poet who understood a great deal that did not come through reading or architecture.

Here's what we know: He received little formal education. He knew very little Latin, the language of religion (not faith) in his day. He disdained physical books and believed that their use by friars, and anyone else for that matter, could—and probably would—quickly lead to haughtiness, laziness, or both. Hence, we are told by historians, Francis was unlearned, anti-intellectual, a man who had little use for "ideas."

Those things being true, then we must say that Francis turned from the ideas one discovers in books primarily because he didn't find them very useful. This is surely another primary reason why Francis remains popular today: he anticipated the worldview that turns away from a cosmic theism that's ultimately relevant only in one's mind, and focuses instead on one's relationship with God in the heart and on the actions of one's life. Religion as theory is far less important than religion as something that turns lives around.

Here, too, is what is missing from the anti-intellectual calculus: Francis didn't read; he listened. He was the product of an oral culture. Listening was the primary means of learning for most people for millennia. There were really no schoolchildren throughout the Middle Ages, and very little formal book learning. Erase the modern image you have of kids sitting behind small desks in rows, with books and notebooks and pens, and a teacher standing at the front of the room. Such a scene didn't exist outside of a monastery— and then the pupils were usually young men in the novitiate, not children—until well into the early modern era. Francis learned through listening, as did all curious people.

Because he was so attentive and observed people closely, he was actually a man with a great storehouse of wisdom. He discussed ideas with people he met. Francis lived at the precise time when universities were first being founded in the cities of Europe. They were too new in his day to have much of a personal effect on him, but the new university in Bologna was close to where Francis lived in Assisi, and it is no coincidence that he chose Bologna as one of the first places to found a community of friars outside Assisi. People interested in ideas were drawn to him.

The three great religions of the world were all built on the foundation of oral teaching, memory, and learning. The Torah, the New Testament, and the Qur'an all began with the spoken word and only later were written down. Beyond their basic scriptures, Jews hold the Oral Torah, collected as Mishnah, to be sacrosanct and essential to Judaism. Many Christians are beginning to ponder something similar for themselves, wondering if the teachings of the early Church mothers and fathers are, in fact, a sort of oral New Testament.

Islam's canon includes a comparable orally derived component. The Prophet Muhammad died in 632, and it was more than a century before many teachings essential to Islam were written down. These teachings go beyond the Qur'an; they are called *hadith*, and all relate in some way or another to what the Prophet saw, said, or otherwise approved of. Interestingly, there is an early tradition that says that hadith were never supposed to be written down. It is said that the Prophet himself did not want them written down or collected in books, insisting that his followers remember these teachings and principles just as they had first been relayed.

THE ULTIMATE "OTHER": ISLAM

In the late medieval worldview the greatest "other" was the follower of Islam. Muslims were the sworn enemies of Christendom. Is it any accident, considering his desire to break down barriers between people, that several years after he founded the Franciscan Order, Francis wanted to travel to the East to meet Muslims face-to-face? His first two attempts failed due to difficulties of travel, but in the summer of 1219 Francis and one of his brothers, a simple man whom we know as Illuminato, made the long journey to the banks of the Nile River.

There they meandered their way through two armies encamped opposite one another. Brother Francis and Brother Illuminato were ridiculed and cursed by the soldiers and knights, many of whom lay bleeding and dying. "May God give you peace," Francis said to them, touching them, asking if they needed anything for their wounds. The friars kept going until they were standing barefoot before the sultan.

Francis surely would have known before that day something of the Muslim view of Jesus: that the Qur'an showed deep respect for Jesus, more so than for any other person in human history. Perhaps he knew that Muslims referred to Jesus with titles such as "Messenger," "Son of Mary," and even "Messiah." And maybe he also knew that they shared a vision of the future kingdom of God and even a return of Jesus (as a Muslim), but that Islam does not hold Jesus to be the Savior or the second member of the Trinity.

This is how it might have happened: Long before he ever journeyed to the Middle East, years before he even began his own conversion, Francis would have heard commercial tradesmen like his father speak of the dangerous heretical religion of the East. He would have heard knights and monks—the men of his grandfather's generation—who had served in and returned from the Second Crusade (1145–1149) tell what little they knew of Islam. He would have heard about the famous sermons given by Peter the Hermit, which proclaimed the apocalyptic end of the world and inspired the knights of the First Crusade a century before Francis was born.

Before journeying to Egypt, Francis would have talked with others who knew something about the place and its people. He would have worried about this people who'd been labeled infidels (people of no faith) by Christians, even though they prayed several times a day. He would have known that Muslims were being killed in the Holy Land, and that they had a holy book that was often burned by crusaders. He would have known, and shuddered at, oft-repeated accounts of crusaders on their way to the Holy Land saying to each other, *Do we have to go all that way in order to find our enemies?* and then rounding up the Jews of a town and putting them all to death if they wouldn't confess Christ.[3]

Very few of the writings of Islamic mystics such as Niffari (d. 965) and Sarraj (d. 988) were translated from Arabic into Latin until the twentieth century. And they certainly weren't translated into Italian in Francis's day! So Francis prepared for his travels not by reading, but by listening and cultivating relationships. When he traveled as a young man with his father to Champagne or Bordeaux on his father's trading routes, he would have met all sorts of characters. He was among French-speaking tradesmen and heard their stories of Gaul and of faraway England. At the outposts and hostels where they spent their evenings he met gentlemen, scoundrels, and pilgrims from places far to the East, such as Damascus, Baghdad, and Constantinople. They spoke of what animated them, far beyond the talk of trade.

So when Francis traveled to Egypt at the height of Christian crusading fervor, he angered nearly every religious leader of his day by asking questions and seeking to understand. *What was there to discuss?* many thought. *A holy war has only one righteous side.* But Francis understood through relationships the sort of things that only a few understand. He possessed an openness that was unique among his contemporaries. It's almost as if Francis couldn't see the differences between himself and the sultan, Malik al-Kamil, nephew of the great Saladin. To Francis, there was no "other."

When Francis left their face-to-face meeting in Egypt in September 1219, he left with nothing. Nothing really happened between Francis and the sultan in any historical sense. No battles were averted, and no one was converted. Afterwards both sides continued to fight. But the sultan had met a different sort of Christian—one who was human first and Christian second—or perhaps both equally and simultaneously. Probably for the first time, he experienced a Christian faithful to the original teachings of Jesus.

However the meeting may have affected the Sultan, the encounter had a lasting effect on Francis. By 1221, when Francis was revising his Rule, he was able to say:

> If any of the brothers wish, by divine inspiration,
> to go among the Muslims and other unbelievers
> . . . [he] should conduct himself . . . in these two
> ways. First, do not create arguments or conten-
> tiousness, but instead, "For the Lord's sake accept
> the authority of every human institution," while
> still confessing yourself to be Christian. Second,
> when you see that it is pleasing to God, announce
> God's Word, so that they might come to believe
> in almighty God: the Father, and Son, and Holy
> Ghost.[4]

This is the message and tone of a man deeply respect-
ful of human beings. There probably is no need to contrast
Francis's words with those of his average contemporary who
preached and believed that Muslims and Jews should simply
confess Jesus Christ or die. I'll spare you those.

One of the most recent scholarly biographers of Francis
even makes the case that Francis's writings show evidence of
his affection and respect for Islam's spiritual practices. For
example, when he asks those in a position of civil authority
to herald the time for daily prayer with a bell or some other easily heard sound, he could be remembering from his
Egyptian sojourn the Muslim call to prayer.[5]

It is not that Francis had a modern understanding of
what every human being deserves: life, liberty, and the pur-
suit of happiness. He was still a medieval man, but he was
different. The twentieth-century philosopher Simone Weil
once observed, erroneously, that "just as the notion of rights
is alien to the Greek mind, so also it is alien to the Christian inspiration whenever it is pure and uncontaminated
by the Roman, Hebraic, or Aristotelian heritage. One cannot imagine St. Francis of Assisi talking about rights."[6] She
clearly didn't have an understanding of what "pure and un-

contaminated" Christian inspiration might be for Francis. It was precisely in his rediscovery of the concern for human rights in Jesus' own teachings that Francis raised the cause of the "other" in the early thirteenth century.

Jesus' teachings were themselves a fresh engagement with the Hebrew prophetic tradition of speaking truth to power and championing the powerless. So, in trying to love by first honoring the rights and freedoms of others and placing everything else second, Francis was acting out of the first principle of ancient Judaism as well as the message of the Gospels.

Less than two years after Francis wrote those peaceful words in his Rule of 1221, the Holy Roman Emperor Frederick II announced his intention to mount the greatest military assault ever upon Islam and Sultan Malik al-Kamil. Frederick pledged that he would even personally lead his knights into battle. One of our greatest scholars of early Franciscan history has concluded that Francis penned his "Praises to God" (1224) to express his profound sadness about this attack: "[L]aid out in simple staccato rhythm, [they] are Francis's personalized version of *The Ninety-Nine Beautiful Names of Allah*." In other words, Francis was so influenced by his travels and understandings of Islam that "Francis is praying in an Islamic mode" when he writes[7]:

> You are love.
> You are wisdom.
> You are humility.
> You are patience.
> You are beauty.
> You are meekness.
> You are a stronghold.
> You are rest.
> You are joy.
> You are hope.

You are justice.
You are all one needs.
You are all the riches we require.
You are beauty.
You are meekness.
You are strength.
You are refreshment.
You are hope.
You are our faith.
You are our only love.
You are all our sweetness.
You are our eternal life.

Medieval Fear of the
Created World as "Other"

The other discarded "other" in the medieval universe into which Francis was born was the created world of animals, birds, insects, plants, and rocks (the solid features of the earth). Early in his conversion, Francis began to realize that he was deeply a part of the rest of Creation rather than apart from it.

One of his earliest religious gestures was to release doves that had been captured and were being offered for sale. Francis begged for them and then let them go. He did the same with fish; when a fisherman friend presented Francis with one just off the hook, the new friar responded by blessing it and releasing it. Surely, people thought these actions bizarre, at least until they came to know Francis better. He understood his role as a creature to be alongside other creatures, and he was able to pause and consider the blessedness of each one.

It's amazing that Francis hasn't gone down in history as a heretic for some of these ideas, particularly his most famous song and prayer, the "Canticle of the Creatures." How did it happen that, despite being a radical departure from traditional Catholic teaching, the "Canticle" has only earned him a reputation for what used to be a more highly regarded word: sentimentality? Francis's concern for the other in the created world was a bold departure from every norm and put him at risk of censure. We read the "Canticle" today as sweet and gentle, but Francis actually put himself on the line when he wrote these words.

Francis was so far ahead of his time in this one area that we have trouble seeing him as a man of his own era when we evaluate his inclusive approach to the created world. No one in the thirteenth century paid any regard or showed concern to animals, other than as a source of labor, transportation, clothing, or food. Actually, the medieval regard for animals had a quite different focus. Many in the Middle Ages feared animals because they were similar enough to human beings to be regarded as dangerous. Legends and superstitions caused many to believe that some animals might once have been human beings, transformed as a result of the devil's influence. With an abundance of mythological creatures like minotaurs and centaurs running around in Virgil's *Aeneid*, not to mention basilisks and other mysterious creatures in the Bible (Jerome's Vulgate) itself, it isn't hard to imagine how that kind of mindset would develop.

Responding to such a view, the early Church father St. Augustine of Hippo bizarrely offered this defense: "We must firmly hold God's power to be omnipotent in all things. The devils can do nothing . . . unless God permits them. Nor can they create anything; they can only cast a changed shape over what God has made, altering it only in appearance. Devils cannot form any soul or body into bestial or brutal members and essences; but they can in an indescribable way carry a person's phantasm in a bodily shape before others . . . while their real bodies lie in another place, still alive, but in a trance much deeper than sleep."[8] What a comfort that must have been! If the great theologian discussed these issues in such strange ways, just imagine how the average Christian imagined the animal world.

Augustine also held a negative view of the physical world in general. For him, the world was that which purposefully keeps us away from God. So a walk in the woods wasn't an opportunity to see some of God's Creation; it was simply a distraction. Birds singing in the trees might turn our attention away from the God we should meet in prayer or study or through the sacraments of the Church. Then, of course, the world of distractions for someone like Augustine also included all women as temptations to men. In startling contrast, Francis embraced the world.

A Vision of Harmony
with All Creation

In reaching out to critters and fowl and fish, not to mention sultans and women, Francis was a man without fear. He didn't see devils behind the eyes of animal creatures, not even in those creatures doing scary animal things. Francis's embracing of animals was a way of looking back to the Garden of Eden, when all Creation lived together in harmony, as well as forward to a future redemption for every living thing.

The anecdotes of Francis with nonhuman creatures are the most endearing of any in his life. Many of these accounts sound implausible, but Francis was unique in his ability to connect with animals and birds, and he showed himself gentle and quiet enough to be nonthreatening to even the tenderest of creatures.

The sound of running water was the mystery that inspired poet William Wordsworth. For Henry David Thoreau, it was the sound of walking in an ancient forest that was his cathedral. The singing of birds was Francis's great inspiration. Their songs didn't just stop him in his tracks to listen, but sparked something in his soul that nothing else could; he heard angels' voices in the chickadee's chant and the mockingbird's caw.

But Francis wasn't reacting against Christianity, as Wordsworth and Thoreau did with their embrace of the natural world. Francis simply understood the Incarnation of God to extend beyond the person of Christ to all things. He looked back to the Garden and believed that Creation was all, still, very good. Francis would never have written, as did the author of *Walden* in a letter to a friend, "Why won't you believe . . . that sometimes in a fluttering leaf, one may hear all your Christianity preached?"[9] There was no either-or. For Francis it was a matter of both-and.

When Francis preached to the birds and sang to the creatures in the wild, he was embracing an ancient view that all created beings are, in some sense, one. He was turning from mainstream Christian thought that had desacralized the natural world and—whether he intended to or not—beginning to reclaim some of the ideas once held by native peoples in Italy. These reached back to the pre-Christian era when Pan was the god of glens, woods, groves, and everything wild. I am not suggesting that he believed that Pan existed as a god of the woods, but Francis sanctified pagan traditions by insisting on a sacramental vision of the natural world. Just as many of the churches of Rome are built atop temples to gods and goddesses, and just as many of the hymns written during the sixteenth century originated as drinking tunes, Francis embraced the claims of pagan stories in terms of our connection to the world around us. These tales were known to children and told of Pan making panpipes out of clusters of reeds to sing of divine mysteries and of the sacredness of trees. The Church had long suppressed any worship or symbols of Pan, but the idea of the divine at play in the created world had never died away.[10]

All creatures are connected, Francis was inspired to discover, for he hadn't learned it in any catechism. He was removing layers of soot from centuries of Catholic theology.

Lex Orandi, Lex Credendi

Any good spiritual director will tell you that your prayers are limited by your image of God. If you cannot imagine God as other than a fearsome judge sitting on a throne, then you will always pray in ways that are like a subject bowing before a king. If you imagine God primarily as a shepherd who seeks lost sheep, you may pray as one who is frequently or easily lost. And so on. Our prayers tend to track with our image of God.

So what exactly does it say about Francis's image of God that he prayed in ways that were so outside the bounds of the theological and spiritual norms of his era? In his care for the creatures of the world, for what a good Buddhist would call "every sentient being," Francis must have shocked, even disappointed, most religious people of his era. Few people today consider the life of a bird, a wolf, a fish, a worm, or a bee to be as precious as a human life. Imagine then how many fewer made this part of their worldview eight hundred years ago.

The late medieval worldview was simple. God was located outside of human beings, outside and above the earth itself. Human beings were seen as trapped: God was above them in the heavens, and forces of evil ruled the world at their feet. A soul was believed to have been pure before it was imprisoned in a body, but now, saddled with a bag of bones, it struggled to do its best and not be too influenced by the appetites and passions of the flesh. A soul was at battle in the world in order to have a hope of heaven when its body's life was over. This view of the world dominated in the summer of 1224, when Francis wrote the "Canticle of the Creatures," just as it did earlier in the Middle Ages.

Listen to that song, and note the new vocabulary he created:

> Most high, almighty, good Lord God,
>   to you belong all praise, glory, honor, and blessing!
>
> To you alone, highest One, they all belong,
>   and no one is worthy to speak your name.
>
> Praised be you, my Lord and God, with all your creatures,
>   and especially our Brother Sun,
>   who brings us the day and the light.
>   He is fair and shines with great splendor:
>   O Lord, he signifies you to us!
>
> Praised be you, my Lord, for our Sister Moon
>   and all the stars:
>   You formed them in the heavens,
>   shining and beautiful!
>
> Praised be you, my Lord, for our Brother Wind,
>   and for air and cloud, and calms and weather
>   through which you uphold life in all creatures.

Praise the Lord for our Sister Water,
    who is very useful to us and humble
    and precious and clean.

Praise the Lord for our Brother Fire,
    through whom you give us light in the darkness.
    He is bright and pleasant and mighty and strong.

Praise the Lord for our Mother Earth,
    who sustains us and keeps us,
    and brings forth the grass and all
    the fruits and flowers of every color.

Praised be you, O Lord, for all who show forgiveness and
    pardon one another for your sake,
    and who endure weakness and tribulation.

Blessed are they who peaceably endure,
    for you, Most High, shall give them a crown.

Praise to you, O Lord, for our Sister Death
    and the death of the body from whom no one may escape.
    Woe to those who die in mortal sin:
    but blessed are they who are found walking by your
    most holy will, for the second death
    shall have no power to do them harm.

Praise to you, O my Lord, and all blessing.
    We give you thanks and serve you with great humility.

No theological degree created those words, that vision. Theological training would actually have gotten in the way. But thanks to Francis, "mysticism became the possession of the people" (to quote Martin Buber referring to a different religious revival—the early Hasidic movement).[11] Francis responded to the otherness of the natural world like a mystic, not a scientist. A later medieval Italian, Leonardo da Vinci, would turn his own interest in animals, water, air, and motion into scientific discoveries. But Francis responded more simply, with gratitude and awe, looking for ways to understand himself in the context of the larger world.

Notice what is absent in Francis's song. There is no mention of Jesus or Christ. There are no theological statements, only praise. He created a new vocabulary with the "Canticle," as well as involving a wider world in divine activity. Had Francis not been so popular among the people of his day, and had his message not resonated so deeply with the *sensus fidei*, "the sense of the faithful," he wouldn't have gotten away with this innovation.[12] Any other wandering mystic and preacher would surely have been censured for talking and not talking about God in this way.

Francis had been raised to believe that the world was a place to be feared and traversed with dread. The allegories in Bunyan's *Pilgrim's Progress* communicate this perspective, which prevailed in Bunyan's seventeenth-century Protestant England just as it did in Francis's thirteenth-century Catholic Italy. The world is referred to as the "City of Destruction," something to flee, and Christian, the protagonist, must struggle and seek his way through earthly obstacles everywhere including places called the "Valley of the Shadow of Death" and the "Slough of Despond," all in an effort to finally reach the "Celestial City," heaven itself. The feeling is that there is nothing to be appreciated on earth itself; earth is a battleground, a minefield, a bear pit.

But to Francis, this is not an evil world aiming to do him harm. He is able to look at it and bless it in each of its constituent parts; he praises and blesses the things of the world around him as his brothers and sisters. And he cares for the sultan, for inanimate objects, even for cold-blooded creatures, not because God tells him to, but because he has grown to understand all Creation as a divine contribution to the authentic human experience. Wind, Water, Fire, Earth, and Death are all tangible evidence of divine omnipresence.

CHAPTER 5

THROUGH PERSONAL POVERTY

Where we explore Francis's personal poverty, which led to the popularity of his spiritual movement during his life, but which proved impossible for his followers to sustain after his death.

I magine yourself walking around Assisi in the year 1212 or 1213. The friars (men and women we've read about, such as Leo, Bernard, and perhaps even Clare), dressed in worn, torn, and discolored castoff cassocks from the monks of nearby Benedictine monasteries, appear in the public square, singing. They arrive unannounced by any religious authority, but rather of their own accord, as might a troupe of traveling theatrical performers.

Your eyes are opened wide by the unexpected joy you see, and your tired spirit is rejuvenated. The playful songs coming from the performers bring a smile to the face of even the most jaded workman and tired mother of ten.

Surrounding the square, behind those gathered, are the Romanesque pillars of what we would call city hall, the courtyard of the bishop's palace, and behind it a small church with doors barred, for it's a weekday at midday. The brothers perform for the people in the square, then preach. Their performance is surprising because it is neither penitential, like that of the wandering ascetics who come through town publicly flogging themselves, nor frivolous, like the pure entertainments of traveling theater. And when the preaching comes, it is perhaps the first time that people really hear the gospel message, for any time they've been in church it has been mostly mumbled and in Latin.

Mendicancy—A New Kind of Religious Life

The popularity of Francis's spiritual movement in the two decades between his conversion and death is almost without precedent in the history of Christianity. Never had a new religious movement expanded as rapidly as his did by the end of its first decade. Other reforms within monasticism had shown quick growth, but not like early Franciscanism. In one of the most pregnant phrases of G. K. Chesterton's genius little book about Francis, he wrote: "What St. Benedict had stored St. Francis scattered." And this scattering was deliberate on Francis's part, as he made the values and spirituality of traditional monasticism available to everyday people everywhere.

The rapid growth happened almost despite Francis himself. On one hand, he invited and accepted just about anyone to join him. That was a radical departure from the norm—for example, from what St. Benedict's Rule advises—and this open admission policy surely became a primary reason for the high numbers. On the other hand, the personal demands that Francis put upon someone to become a true friar were enormous.

Consider the contrast between the first half century of the Cistercian reform one hundred years earlier in France and the first twenty years of Franciscanism. Beginning in the closing years of the eleventh century, Cistercian reform was designed to return Benedictine monasticism to the Rule of St. Benedict. Monastic houses had strayed far from some of Benedict's principles of daily work, fixed-hour prayer, and hospitality; and clericalism had run amok. The monks in Citeaux (the Latin translation of which inspires the name "Cistercian") wanted to follow every jot and tittle of St. Benedict's original inspiration. Led by men such as Robert of Molesme, and made famous a generation later by Bernard of Clairvaux, the Cistercian reform resulted in dozens of new and reformed monastic houses all over France in less than a decade. Within another twenty-five years, there were more than three hundred transformed Cistercian monasteries as far afield as Norway, Ireland, and Poland.[1]

Francis knew Benedictines firsthand, and he knew Cistercians. Surely, he had heard some of the sermons and prayers of Bernard of Clairvaux, who was formally canonized just a few years before Francis's birth. So he knew that bringing changes to revered monastic traditions was nothing new.

The Cistercian spirit of work appealed to Francis. He appreciated their return to a focus on manual labor, taking monks out of choir and scriptorium and into God's Creation. The Cistercians created a vast agrarian economy, and the farm work was done by a new class of monks not mentioned in Benedict's Rule, called *conversi*, or "lay brothers." Francis loved the spiritual egalitarianism of valuing every brother in an order regardless of his ability to read, study, or sing. (In fact, the debate continues as to whether Francis was himself anything more than a lay brother. Most experts agree that he was akin to what we today would call an ordained deacon. He was certainly never a priest, and he didn't desire to be one.)

Although the Cistercian idea was a way of welcoming more people into monastic life, ultimately *conversi* were meant to toil so that choir monks could pray and study. Within Francis's movement, lay brothers would become the norm, not the exception, and they did not hold positions of lesser spiritual importance.

Also contrary to the Cistercian reforms, Francis wasn't interested in the results of all that monastic labor. What Cistercians valued as self-sufficiency, he called storing up treasures on earth. Following the example of Jesus, he wanted none of that, so despite how foolish it might have looked to others, he refused to plan for even the most immediate future needs of his community of men. Francis was much closer in spirit and practice to Norbert of Xanten, who started a community of reforming monastics in a valley near Laon, France, in 1120. Norbert's monks performed manual labor as a virtue in and of itself and remained deliberately poor.

Poverty became, for Francis, a way of discovering his identity before God. As Pope Francis recently said, in reference to the famous parable of the rich man and Lazarus, "The rich man in the Gospel has no name, he is simply 'a rich man.' Material things, his possessions, are his face. He has nothing else."[2]

Francis wanted to be a mendicant, not a monk. A mendicant was a voluntarily poor Christian who relied on the goodness of others, or on God's grace, for daily needs. The Franciscan Order is one of three mendicant orders that arose almost simultaneously in Western Europe; the Dominicans and the Carmelites are the other two. Such orders were populated by men and women who wanted to follow Christ in greater simplicity than traditional monastic orders seemed to allow. They wanted to be poor the way Christ was poor.

Mendicants also held another value in esteem that is almost the polar opposite of what is taught in the Rule of St. Benedict. Whereas a Benedictine or Cistercian took a vow of stability—a solemn intention to remain within a particular monastery or convent under the authority of a certain abbot or abbess—a mendicant vowed faithfulness to the principles of mendicancy.

Mendicancy was a way of raising impermanence to a virtue as Jesus had done when he praised the lilies of the field for not worrying about tomorrow (Mt 6:28). Families were the basic unit of the medieval economy, and mendicant friars left their families behind—not for safety in cloisters, but for a more dangerous life of discipleship. Simply being "on the road" carried with it potential danger: nearly half of all murders in the late Middle Ages took place on the highways and outside of towns.

The life of the friar was ideally suited for towns—city centers—which became more abundant in the century before Francis's birth. People began to urbanize in order to realize political, economic, social, religious, and cultural benefits. Universities were being born. Towns became places of destination and identity, organized around a common trade such as textiles or ceramics, and often with regular markets and other organized reasons to gather aside from church. So to cities the friars flocked.

A New Economy

There they met merchants, burghers (the class of men prepared to be city officials—*bourgeoisie*), and craftsmen making a living away from the old agrarian system. These urban occupations presented men and women with something that hadn't existed roughly from the end of the Roman Empire until sometime in the late eleventh century: cash and coin.

The florin, late medieval Italy's most recognized coin, was first struck with West African gold twenty-six years after Francis's death in Florence. It remains an icon of the Italy of Dante and Petrarch, with an image of St. John the Baptist on one side and a lily on the other. But before the florin, nearly every hill town had its own coinage. They were all silver, but each was distinctive. Some were larger in size, or *grosso*; and some smaller, or *piccolo*. Large or small, they clanged in the silk purses of merchants and jingled even in the cassock pockets of monks.

Francis disliked the money economy. He disliked the system whereby the poor would come, increasingly in times of famine or other need, to ask for handouts of money from wealthy monks. He didn't even want his friars to handle money. Somehow, if the Gospel was to come alive in people's lives, the ways that money was being used had to change.

Francis thought that coin itself—representing the economy of buying and selling—was the problem. He even scolded his friars (the textual tradition uses the euphemistic phrase, "with great intensity of spirit") for attempting to purchase food for the evening meal while visiting a nearby town. They'd reported back to Francis saying that nothing was available. "You didn't find anything because you trust in your flies, that is, in your coins, and not in God," he fired back at them. Then he told them to go back and beg, without anything in their pockets, and they'd find success.[3]

Much has been written about how parts of Europe transitioned rapidly from a feudal society to an urban economy in the eleventh and twelfth centuries. We don't need to lay all of that out here, but we should pause to consider how Francis was a part of this transition. He was raised in an urban economy himself. He knew what it was to own, to buy, and to sell at a profit. And he made the cardinal principle of membership in his mendicant order the renunciation of what many valued most in his century: their newfound ability to own, buy, and sell.

If you own things, then you have to protect them, he said. And if you have to protect them, you may then even be tempted to use violence against someone. And Francis never wanted to do that. So he sought to live a life "open" before others, making both himself and his worldly things available. Just as he decided to take no ownership of property or things in his Rule and form of life, Francis didn't see his life as his own property either. He was inspired by the Beatitudes.

A Desire to Be Small

Blessed are the poor in spirit . . . the meek . . . the pure in heart, for they will see God," Jesus said (Mt 5:3–8). For Francis, taking these teachings seriously meant that poverty doesn't always and only relate to money, or the lack of it. He was sensitive to other ways of "being poor" as well. He believed that a friar—and any true follower of Christ—was to be insignificant in all of the ways in which the world measures success. For this reason, he was unmoved by those who thought that the Church needed to become more powerful.

A century before Francis's birth, Pope Gregory VII (1073–1085) instituted reforms that wrested control from secular authorities—principally, the Holy Roman Emperor—to ensure that ecclesiastical appointments, such as bishops and abbots, would be made by the Church and not the state. (This struggle is being quietly reenacted today between the Vatican and the Chinese government over ecclesiastical hierarchy in mainland China.) But to Francis's mind and spirit, such reforms were nonessential, for they involved power and authority, neither of which were values he prioritized.

One reason why it took eight hundred years for a pope to take the name Francis is that every man who has been elected since the early thirteenth century has known that Francis didn't support the idea of one of his own becoming a man with great power. One of the earliest biographies has Francis saying to the future Pope Gregory IX, while St. Dominic is standing nearby, "Lord, my brothers are called *minors* so that they will not presume to become greater. Their vocation teaches them to remain in a lowly station and to follow the footsteps of the humble Christ."[4] He believed that even a bishop's chair was too "high" for a true Franciscan to sit upon. This is another meaning of the word *poverty*: low, or small. The name that Francis used for his fledgling order (he never called his followers "Franciscans") was *Fraticelli*, or Little Brothers. This was amended in Latin to *Ordo Fratrum Minorum*, or the Order of Friars Minor. Their founder intended that he and his fellow friars be, quite literally, small.

Counterpoising this intended diminutiveness was the leader of the Catholic Church when Francis first formed his band of brothers, Pope Innocent III (1198–1216). Never before had a pope taken so much power for himself or demanded so much respect for his office. He was a politician and diplomat more than a churchman, but he played all of these roles extremely successfully. Born into one of the noblest families of Rome, Innocent III was born to become pope, but also trained as a theologian and lawyer in Paris. He was shrewd.

Innocent III had approved and tried to organize the various mendicant orders of ragtag men throughout Western Europe who emerged, preaching the Gospel from town to town, in the decade before Francis's conversion got underway. Some of his advisors encouraged him to squash these groups, as they posed a threat to the power of the papacy by questioning its excesses. But Innocent III was smart. He realized that the mendicants could help him maintain control rather than hurt him, if they urged people toward more peaceful lives and faithfulness to the Gospel. A faithful people may be a more submissive people.

Surely Innocent III must have realized that Francis of Assisi was his spiritual antithesis. It is almost as if he'd read Sun Tzu's *The Art of War* to inspire him to be close to the tiny new friar. Keep your enemies close at hand so that you'll always know what they are doing, wrote the ancient Chinese sage.

What Innocent III was rapidly building for himself and the papacy would last for centuries until the dramatic crisis that faced the Church in the early sixteenth century. He acquired riches, built bureaucracy, repressed opposition, and dominated whenever and however he could. Francis believed that a Catholic and a follower of Christ should do differently. He taught the opposite of what was easily observed in Rome: humility, simplicity, and joyful downward mobility.

One of the tragedies of history is that we no longer possess the original Rule that Francis composed and carried to Rome, seeking Pope Innocent III's approval. Historians have guessed at it, but not even a fragment of the original remains. Most likely, that first Rule was little more than Bible verses woven together with simple exhortations—all about poverty.

WAS FRANCIS *REALLY* POOR?

Since Francis was small and insignificant in appearance, he was considered a pauper by all who saw him," *The Little Flowers* states, relaying an anecdote from the first few years of his ministry. In other words, Francis didn't have to try as hard as some of his brothers to look the part of the poor friar. He wasn't tall, good-looking, or commanding of presence. He was small and somewhat swarthy, and carried himself humbly. In that same story from *The Little Flowers*, we hear Francis trying to convince one of his brothers that the cast-off scraps of bread they've just received are something valuable:

> "This is exactly what I consider a treasure," Francis replied. "Nothing we have here required the work of others. Everything here has been provided for us by God. I think we should ask God to help our hearts to see the treasures of this—examples of holy poverty at work."[5]

In this statement we find three keys to understanding how Francis characterized living out voluntary poverty in one's life: not taking from the labor of others; recognizing everything received as from God; and seeking a change of inner vision, not simply external circumstances, status, or possessions.

There were many working poor in Francis's Middle Ages, just as there are in our day. They were poor in the sense that they had little or no ability to do things like change occupation or move from one place to another. They had to work hard to scrape by. They had no security beyond the proximity of family.

But Francis wasn't talking about the working poor when he began to praise the nobility of poverty. He was talking about emulating those who are more literally paupers—owning nothing beyond what they have upon their backs. Here is medieval expert Michel Mollat's definition of what it meant to be a *pauper*:

> A pauper was a person who permanently or temporarily found himself in a situation of weakness, dependence, or humiliation, characterized by the privation of the means to power and social esteem (which means varied with period and place): these included money, relations, influences, power, knowledge, skill, nobility of birth, physical strength, intellectual capacity, and personal freedom and dignity. Living from hand to mouth, he had no chance of rising without assistance.[6]

Francis read the teachings of Jesus and saw that Jesus spoke of how easily these sorts of people were able to understand God; he became a pauper willingly in order to discover what it is about complete poverty that provides an easier path to knowing God. He insisted that the friars never own anything, never receive or handle money, never work for a wage, always beg for their daily bread, and abide by a host of other measures to ensure that they remained needy. Possessions were not to come between them and God.

"Blessed are the poor," says Christ in Luke's Gospel, and "Blessed are the poor in spirit," in Matthew's. To be destitute is never a virtue or blessing in and of itself, but it allows for the cultivation of essential virtues such as humility when worldly opportunities and cares are intentionally removed from one's life.

Thomas of Celano paints the picture with a vivid example from daily life: how Francis instructed the brother cook not to soak beans the night before he intended to serve them to the friars, "as people usually do. This was so the brothers would observe the words of the holy Gospel: 'Do not be concerned about tomorrow.'" So Friar Cook learned to start beans in the morning after Morning Prayer.[7]

Still, there are those who thought then, and there are those who believe now, that all of these machinations around voluntary poverty were somehow foolish, even disingenuous. A decade ago a college professor in California, for instance, wrote a book arguing that, having been born into money, power, and influence, Francis couldn't have understood what it meant to be truly poor, despite giving away all he possessed and living the way he did. He argues:

> For when Francis, on that fateful day in the bishop's chamber, suddenly removed his clothes and handed them over to his disgruntled father, he did so with the expectation that by renouncing his patrimony here on earth he would become the heir to an even greater, albeit spiritual, fortune in heaven. Moreover, in his pursuit of these heavenly treasures, Francis managed to win the admiration and even veneration of other Christians whom he made feel guilty about their own involvement in this world, thus transforming himself into one of the most influential men of his day.[8]

This unfortunate interpretation ignores Francis's overt, continuous intention, spoken and lived, to remain in humility and poverty. When Francis faced his father that day on the Piazza Vescovado in front of the bishop, it is true that he made a grand gesture of returning everything to him, even his clothes. He was surely conscious of the dramatic effect of his actions, but beyond that he wouldn't have had any other great expectation. Francis voluntarily became a true pauper, and it was years before he reaped any "reward" from it. He was perceived, in fact, as an absolute fool. He was cast out by his friends, by his family, by everyone he knew. Children threw clods of dirt at him and at his brother friars because they looked and behaved so strangely. The people of his hometown regarded the early converted Francis as nothing more than an idiot, a simpleton, a heretic—sometimes all three.

From 1205 to 1209 Francis's actions were simple steps of a very simple sort of obedience. He was like a man who had been asleep and was suddenly awakened by a voice from heaven. He heard that "voice" in his heart and in the Gospels, and it told him to give away everything, including his dignity.

To imply that renouncing his father before the bishop would instantly give Francis power and influence is naïve at best, and deliberately inaccurate at worst. And the notion that he would have felt confident of gaining heaven by renouncing everything doesn't make sense either. First of all, this assumes a certainty of belief in Francis that is more characteristic of twentieth- and twenty-first-century Protestants than it ever was of thirteenth-century Catholics. Second, in the minds of the people of Assisi, who was Francis modeling himself after in doing what he did? Not so much Jesus as the Waldensians and the Cathars—two earlier mendicant groups who were periodically deemed heretics during Francis's lifetime. And heretics, by definition, do not go to heaven.

The Difficulty of True Poverty

His poverty-loving had an activist flavor about it. Francis learned to take care of what he used and consumed, assuming that another might need what one does not use. He practiced this careful use of material goods and taught his brothers to do the same—often to their sincere frustration. For living so close to the bone is difficult.

So it is not surprising that after Francis's death his friars gradually went from being deliberately *small* to, for lack of a better word, *fat*; they disregarded Francis's principles, particularly those regarding personal poverty. This is why when people hear the word *friar* today, what pops into their imaginations is someone altogether different from the person of Francis of Assisi. Most likely the image is of Friar Tuck, the fat, jolly, foolish companion of Robin Hood according to English legend. Tuck came to represent the friar in the popular imagination.

Similar tales of overindulged friars appear in *Gargantua and Pantagruel*, a series of bestselling novels written by Francois Rabelais, a French monk-turned-critic of the mid-sixteenth century. By then, fatuous friars who indulged in food and drink and told ribald, scatological tales were assumed to be the widespread norm. This shift did not happen by accident or by malevolent design, but because too many real-life friars had begun, after Francis's death, to live lives that didn't resemble their founder's.

What went wrong? How did this happen? Why was personal, voluntary poverty the first Franciscan virtue to be abandoned?

There's no reason to get out a soapbox and preach faithfulness to Francis's ideals. They are so rarely imitated because they are so demanding.

Christ's first followers faced the same difficulty, for Francis's voluntary poverty was just what Jesus taught 1,200 years earlier. The simple answer is that, to echo and rephrase the quote from G. K. Chesterton above, Christian ideals have not failed so much as they've never really been tried. Still, there are moments in history when the ideal becomes real, and when it does, the message of the Gospel suddenly makes obvious, tangible sense. Francis crystallized one of those moments in the two decades of his ministry.

CHAPTER 6

BY DEVELOPING A NEW
SPIRITUALITY

*Where we see that Francis lived at a time
when the Church felt threatened by individual expressions of faith, yet he created
ways for ordinary people to mark their
lives as holy.*

Perhaps my favorite Francis story of all is the one that
shows him resisting the attempts of a younger friar to
obtain his own prayer book.

The young man has recently joined the order and is
growing in fervor daily. He does not speak often to Francis,
for even though Francis is eminently approachable, the friars are good about leaving him alone when it comes to many
of the smaller details. So, when the boy wants his own prayer
book, he begins by approaching the friar who is directing
his spiritual growth. This mentor tells him no—everyone
knew that Francis established a rule saying individual friars
shouldn't need to own their own prayer books.

The young man decides that his need is sincere and ur-
gent, that he is growing so rapidly in faith and loves to pray

so much, that to be without his own breviary is an unnecessary hardship.

"May I have one?" he pleads to Francis one day.

"Please don't," Francis replies.

"But why not?" the young man asks.

"Because *here* is your breviary. *Here* is your breviary!" Francis repeats, pointing his finger at the young man's heart.

Back in the year 1200, there was no such thing as *spirituality*. The word didn't exist. In fact, spirituality didn't exist until about the beginning of the twentieth century. People talked about religion, religious obligations, and religious life, rather than something called spirituality. To distinguish between religious life and spirituality is a modern differentiation.

This is not to say that there was no sense of individuality in the Middle Ages. This major fallacy has been around for a long time: the false idea that medieval men and women had no concept of their own personal and individual identity, that they never considered their feelings and faith apart from their societal place or family unit, and that a personal relationship with God (occurring independent of worship in church) was a foreign concept. One has only to read St. Augustine's *Confessions*—a fourth-century text—in order to see that this couldn't possibly be true. There was no lack of individuality and individual understanding throughout the Middle Ages. People were just as brazen, arrogant, self-centered, and self-destructive back then as we are today—they certainly felt that they had the agency to do as they willed, just as we do today.

People have always known that they are unique, and they've always sensed and sought faith, one by one, powerfully and individually, with the Divine. But there have definitely been times in history when people have had fewer opportunities to express that uniqueness. The medieval Church offered few outlets for people to express an emotional or personal experience of God. And when people did, it was viewed as dangerous—as if personal expressions of faith would somehow diminish the Church's authority. Francis didn't seem to hold this view, but he often didn't share the concerns of traditional ecclesiastical leaders. If the vocabulary had existed in the early thirteenth century, Francis would have said that one of the primary purposes of his work was to help people to access their own spirituality.

DIFFERENT WAYS OF UNDERSTANDING THE WORLD

The popular dualist perspective that existed in the century before Francis was that God and Satan were at war with each other in the world we walk about in. There was Good and there was Evil and they were opposing forces. This idea, known as Manichaeism, was named for Mani, the third-century Persian prophet who first originated the teachings. Light was opposed to darkness, and the incorporeal (spiritual) was in opposition to the corporeal (bodily). Manichaean belief was Gnostic, in that secret truths were thought to be accessible only to those initiated into "seeing" them by renouncing the world. Think of every good science fiction novel you've ever read, or every popular myth that includes a battle and triumph over darkness, and you have a sense of how people viewed the battle within their physical lives.

Even close to Francis, for instance, there was a religious movement right around the time of his childhood, mostly in southern France, called the Cathars. I mentioned them in passing in the last chapter. They embodied this sort of dualism in everyday ways. Their view of the present world was that it was inexplicably and unavoidably engulfed by darkness. They felt the struggle between evil and good as an intimate one. Every time something bad happened in life, they felt the hand of the Evil One upon their shoulders and knew that God was unable to do anything about it. There was "this world" and "the world to come," and they believed that what God wanted was for his people to put their minds and hearts on the world to come, since this one was only fallen and dark.

As a result, the Cathars put little value on human life. They did many troubling things that are unnecessary to recount in detail here. The first pope to meet the converted Francis, Innocent III, found the Cathars so troubling that he originated what became a brutal crusade, sending soldiers and mercenaries under the papal seal to kill them, lest they infiltrate and influence the Church with their insidious ideas even more than they had already.

Both the Cathars' teaching and way of living, and this pope's response to it would have troubled Francis. Darkness was compounded by darkness. But most of all, Francis simply didn't understand dualism because it wasn't an accurate depiction of the world he lived in. When Francis walked in and looked around the world, he saw the good—relationships, music, work, creatures—and he experienced the beauty and love that overcome ugliness and hatred when people strive toward goodness rather than darkness. For Francis there was little separation between earth and heaven—to him earth, as the saying goes, was full of heaven. And not only did he demonstrate an understanding of the world that was different from that of most of his contemporaries, but his fresh worldview impacted his understanding of sin.

Spiritual Practices

A big change in Church teaching about sin had occurred gradually between the fourth and twelfth centuries. Augustine, who ruled the Christian theological roost throughout the Middle Ages, taught that sin was introduced in the Garden of Eden and that since then it has been hereditary, passed on by procreation from parent to child. Sin, he said, was life-altering and unavoidable.

Several centuries later, theologians like Anselm and Abelard taught that sin was less akin to marrow in the bones, and more comparable to the work of the heart. Sin came to be understood as a voluntary action inspired by desire, temptation, and will rather than an essential structure of human life.

One result of this change in perspective was a dramatic rise in asceticism. A sinful condition breeds obligation, and a tendency to sin breeds hope that personal vigilance can make a difference. So Christians began to "discipline" their bodies in the hope that their "hearts" would learn not to sin. Also, since sin was no longer understood to be quite so inevitable, by Francis's day people had begun to count every sin in their lives. In Augustine's theological era, Christians thought of sin like skin—it surrounded you and was an absolutely necessary part of life. But by 1200, sin seemed more akin to a mysterious disease, dangerous but possibly curable.

This new approach to sin created the need for spiritual practice. Francis understood sin and the Christian life in terms more like Anselm and Abelard than Augustine; he sought to teach his heart to desire holier things and to train himself to sin less. Many of Francis's writings are to encourage himself and others in the way of personal conversion. Spirituality and spiritual practice became essential.

One example of Francis's emphasis on spirituality is his vision of partaking of Communion as less a religious obligation than a way of keeping close to God. That was uncommon. One scholar recounts an anecdote that represents the general attitude toward the Eucharist throughout the Middle Ages:

> The custom for priests and monks to carry the Eucharist with them on their journeys persisted for many centuries. St. Ambrose recorded in his sermon *De Excessu Fratris sui Satyri* (375) how his brother Satyrus, who was still a catechumen, feared for his life in a shipwreck, and asked a companion who was carrying the Sacrament to give it to him. On receiving it, he wrapped it round his neck in a piece of linen, and threw himself into the sea: "not fearing death, but rather that he should die without the mystery . . ." On reaching safety he desired Baptism and Communion, "for having found the heavenly Mystery wrapped in a napkin such a protection, he know not what blessing he might not expect."[1]

Today we might call such an approach superstitious; while Francis wouldn't have called it that, he clearly desired a richer understanding of the Eucharist. He speaks in his "Testament" of the Eucharist as the primary symbol of God's incarnation in our lives. In the months before his death, the man who had become renowned for finding God in creatures, suddenly wrote, "I can plainly see, here in this world, the Son of God only in his most holy Body and Blood, which the priests alone receive and administer."[2]

But most profound is the context in which Francis urges everyone (not just vowed friars) who desires to follow gospel principles to receive Communion throughout the year. In the 1210 "First Rule of the Third Order," for ordinary Christians, he wrote: "All should make a confession of their sins three times a year and receive Communion at Christmas, Easter, and Pentecost. They should be reconciled with their neighbors and restore what belongs to others."[3] In other words, the Eucharist is meant to be at the center of Christian life.

Francis's writings are in fact full of efforts to bring spirituality into the lives, work, homes, and churches of Christians. Another means for Francis of growing close to God was praying the Liturgy of the Hours, those daily prayers that were originally designed for and required of all priests. He encouraged all who desired to live according to Franciscan principles, even if they could not take the vows of a friar, to pray the seven hours of the Divine Office daily. Prayer thus became a means of talking with God in the words that King David first used long ago as a shepherd in the hills building his own relationship with God. A number of stories about Francis show him stopping to pray while walking from one town to the next, and the prayer stops always seem more joyful than obligatory.

Many other spiritual practices fill Francis's teachings and life, and they are not the province of vowed friars only. He taught men and women to dress humbly. He explained how fasting could be part of a regular diet. He encouraged people to be thankful by praying before family meals. And he preached nonviolence, urging for example that men never even take up a weapon in their hands.[4]

Hospitality, too, became a virtuous practice learned by the first Franciscans through a series of real-life object lessons—as people knocked on the door or as needs were presented on the street. They opened their doors (though sometimes their living quarters didn't actually have doors) to anyone who came and was interested in their way of life.

All of these spiritual practices were essential to their lives but uncommon in the Middle Ages.

Spirituality vs. Religion

I am seeking the truth not laying it down," wrote Michel de Montaigne, the sixteenth-century French Catholic thinker, at the beginning of an essay on prayer. Montaigne detested religious dogmatism and fanaticism more than anything else, and he lived in a century that saw plenty of it. Well, so did Francis three centuries earlier. While spurning traditional book learning—for it brought with it a whole host of attitudes and posturings that were anathema to him—Francis became a man of spiritual wisdom. He chose few words to study, and then he did more than study them: he became them.

We see in Francis's writings an attempt to recapture the core of Jesus's teachings in practical ways, but also a reaching back to the mystical element of Christian faith that had been lost in the regular activity of churches and in the political maneuverings of cardinals, bishops, and the Curia in Rome. He placed such a priority on personal prayer, contemplation, charity, and loving-kindness because the habits of the heart are important to God, as well as to the faithful who want to know God better. He was an eminently practical mystic who was always attempting to balance spirituality with religion. This is why young friars were taught how to pray earnestly and often, yet asked not to want their own prayer books.

Spirituality and religion needn't be opposed to each other, but Francis lived at a time when the Church felt threatened by individual expressions of faith. Priests were taught that they were the primary mediators between God and their parishioners; without the sacraments there was little access to God that made religious sense in the Middle Ages. In many ways, Francis changed all of that.

Just imagine what the priests, bishops, and Church hierarchy thought when they first heard that Francis was creating a branch of his religious order for men and women who would remain in the world, staying committed to their work, marriages, and responsibilities, while taking on the practices of Franciscan spirituality as a way of knowing God more deeply. The Third Order was born probably in 1210.

Francis offered these ordinary believers interested in a spiritual life their own Rule that provided guidance on ordinary aspects of living, including many of the principles and practices mentioned above, plus gathering together as a community of faith, aiding the sick, and caring for those who die. All of these practices began to be understood anew, as religious/spiritual acts available to everyone, yet only some of them required a priest or church.

It's appropriate here to acknowledge that Francis has never been Rome's favorite religious leader. Indeed, he was a threat to the power of the Church. And the feeling was mutual: Francis wasn't always pleased with the Church either. To see this clearly, consider for example what Francis did and did not do in relation to Church hierarchy. How often do we see him going to Rome to seek the advice of the pope and the Roman Curia? After 1209, when his movement was underway—hardly ever.

In contrast, his exact contemporary, St. Dominic, the founder of the Dominicans, must have known every lemonade vendor on the Via Flaminia, the ancient Roman road that he traveled dozens of times from points north, across the Apennine Mountains, down to the capital. It is really not until the final five or six years of Francis's life, after he had lost control of his own order, that the Franciscans began asking the Pope to intercede frequently on their behalf. By 1225 and 1226, Pope Honorius III was often extending privileges and protections for the friars, as well as raising money for their efforts by assessing fines on others—efforts that Francis wouldn't have supported, let alone requested.[5]

There is also the matter of the Fifth Crusade, which Pope Innocent III began calling for in 1208. In April 1213, he issued a papal bull insisting that all of Christendom support a universal effort to recapture Jerusalem from Muslim control. What did Francis do to support this papal appeal? Nothing. And when Innocent III restated his desires in the most incontrovertible terms two years later at the worldwide Fourth Lateran Council, not only was Francis, the leader of the fastest growing spiritual movement in Europe, not present in Rome, but he ignored the orders the second time around, as well.

Once the religious war was in full swing, Francis actually crossed to the opposing side in order to meet and dialogue with the Sultan Malik al-Kamil. That was in 1219, by which time Oliver of Cologne and William the Count of Holland had joined the forces of King Andrew II of Hungary and Duke Leopold VI of Austria to fight the Muslims on Jerusalem's doorstep. The Fifth Crusade ended in Christian defeat in 1221.

Francis's quiet subversion of papal authority is surely another reason why no pope took the name Francis until 2013. Those on the inside of Church politics have long known that Francis is not a name closely associated with the sort of reverence for papal authority that comes with names such as Peter, John, and Benedict. Francis was never a disobedient son of the Church, but he was a nonconformist who had his own priorities. As a professor at the University of Tübingen, long before he even became a bishop, Joseph Ratzinger (later Pope Benedict XVI) wrote, "Francis's no to that type of Church could not be more radical. It is what we would call a prophetic protest."[6] A Church that owned half of the land in all Europe—which it did under Innocent III—was not one that was devoted to the principles Francis laid out in his Rule of Life for ordinary people.

In 1955, Abraham Joshua Heschel wrote, "When faith is completely replaced by creed, worship by discipline, love by habit; when faith becomes an heirloom rather than a living fountain; when religion speaks only in the name of authority rather than with the voice of compassion—its message becomes meaningless."[7] Francis would have agreed. His own life's work was to fix just these sorts of problems in the Church of his day. This is why early Franciscanism was infused with spirituality and spiritual practice, even when it might have been perceived as competing with what was happening in the churches.

To facilitate spirituality, Francis taught people how to practice their spirituality wherever they were. He loved short, simple, repetitive prayers, and taught them to people who knew little of prayer other than what they heard from the mouth of the priest a few times each year. He asked his brothers to keep the traditional liturgical hours of prayer wherever they happened to be, and he taught everyone he met some simple explanations of each of the phrases of the Our Father. He knew that faith, in order to flame, had to be kindled with close attention. And, of course, somehow he felt empowered to create the friar when Europe was already full of monks. What gave Francis the chutzpah to say that a person could live like a monk outside the confines of a cloister? Further, what made him think that people could live like friars even if they were married and had jobs in the world?

The Age of the Spirit

Francis doesn't exactly tell us where that empowerment came from. He did not keep a diary, recording his personal thoughts so that we could dissect them centuries later. In fact, no one kept diaries and journals back then, and handwriting itself was uncommon. A poet might compose and sing beautiful verses, but handwriting was akin to a craft in the late Middle Ages. It wasn't until centuries later, when people began to believe that children should learn to form letters and sentences, that diaries and personal writing became commonplace.

But Francis was most likely a student of the ideas of a Calabrian prophet who lived a century earlier by the name of Joachim of Fiore. Joachim was a monk and abbot who wrote many books, but never quite fit in the existing orders and structures of the Church. He was a historiographer, a philosopher of history, who began to posit an interesting theory derived from a close "reading" of the history of humanity itself.

The world, Joachim said, had already moved through two massive stages: the "Age of the Father," marked by what is recorded in the Hebrew Bible as God's covenant with the people of Israel; and the "Age of the Son," marked by the incarnation of Christ in the world and the birth of the Christian Church. The second age was about to come to an end, he prophesied. The third and final stage in the history of humanity would be the "Age of the Spirit," according to Joachim. Then we would relate to God in a whole new way.

In the formative years of the Franciscan movement, even while Francis was still alive, there were people who said that Francis and his friars were a tangible sign that Joachim's prophesied Age of the Spirit was dawning. Francis himself may have thought that this was so, though he made no such claim. He may have made certain decisions consciously appealing to God the Holy Spirit more than to God the Father or God the Son. Over and over, we see him seeking gifts and inspiration that are marked by the Spirit. In fact, Francis's spiritual practice is often marked by everyday and ordinary inspiration and an interior spiritual life that doesn't rely closely upon the sacramental life of the Church. Rather than appeal to authority for knowledge of God's will, he often acts boldly and unilaterally as if God's desires are available to him, and to others, by some other means.

Of course the danger of prophecies is also their strongest appeal: they are articulated in terms that can be both universally applied and divergently interpreted. Pope Innocent III, for instance, claimed that the prophecies of Joachim of Fiore were fulfilled by his forces' conquering of Constantinople, the capital city of Eastern Christendom's Byzantine Empire, in a violent crusade. This battle occurred in 1204, the year before Francis's conversion began.[8] Francis would make no claims of his own to fulfilling anything in Joachim. But to many, his spiritual movement was on the leading edge of the third and final stage in the history of humanity.

There are some who have been thinking about and praying for the advent of the Age of the Spirit in our own day, as we've been hearing the words of Pope Francis and being reminded of both Joachim's prophecy and Francis of Assisi's life. In Pope Francis's first apostolic exhortation (a fancy way of saying "papal pep talk") we hear echoes of Francis and that desire for fresh air in the Church:

> I prefer a Church which is bruised, hurting and
> dirty because it has been out on the streets, rath-
> er than a Church which is unhealthy from being
> confined and from clinging to its own security.[9]

It appears that he is talking about a Church that is at times unpredictable, which is threatening to some. But it is a Church that is listening to the Spirit in the same way that Francis sought to listen to the Spirit in his own day.

The novelist and poet Robert Penn Warren once wrote: "We do not know that we have the Truth. But we must have it."[10] This sort of paradox goes a long way toward summarizing how Francis related to God and guided his spiritual life. He didn't simply receive what was spiritually given as if everything had been decided long ago. To Francis, God was fiery, beautiful, transforming, and alive, and he lived as one who learned what God wanted from him each day, sometimes with surprises.

Even the greatest theologian the Church has ever seen, Thomas Aquinas, who lived a generation after Francis, eventually put down his pen and left his great theological work unfinished. He did this because of a spiritual experience he had late in life. He knew that he couldn't say all that needed to be said, nor could he ever understand God fully. At a certain point, even a great theologian realizes that knowledge ceases and love must take over.

Francis believed that a personal spiritual life was essential for knowing God, that ultimately God must be experienced firsthand, and he lived out his belief. Other people—including your priest, the Church, and the friends who are walking beside you—will help you to discern what's true, he said. In fact, Francis was always deliberate in requesting a vicar or counselor for himself—someone to whom he would confess and who would willingly and forthrightly correct him, when necessary. But ultimately, he knew that one has to cultivate a direct relationship with our God who is alive and active and always open to new possibilities.

CHAPTER 7

THROUGH GENTLENESS
AND CARE FOR CREATURES

*Where we learn that Francis was almost
Buddhist in his gentle attention to, not
just people and creatures, but things.*

Francis's life would not have been as interesting to others as it clearly was from the moment he died if he hadn't been a unique lover of people.

He didn't become the world's most popular saint because he founded a religious order. How many books, by contrast, have been written about St. Dominic, who also founded a religious order in the early thirteenth century? Relatively few. Francis wasn't fascinating simply because he was an important religious leader during a challenging time, for St. Augustine was an important religious leader during the Fall of Rome, and who was collecting tales from his life in the years after Augustine's death? No one.

The attraction did not come from the fact that Francis was a writer of vernacular poetry. Such a gift was not highly valued in his day, nor was it in the centuries immediately afterwards, for we know almost nothing about Geoffrey

Chaucer, who lived after Francis and wrote a hundred times more. Similarly, no one was rushing to tell William Shakespeare's life story immediately after his death; if they had, we'd know much more than we in fact know about him, which is almost nothing.

We know a great deal about Francis, by comparison, because he was a great lover of people.

But *love* has too many conflicting meanings, and the word doesn't fully express what Francis did. To use a word with other possibilities, I would clarify that Francis was a man who *cared*. *Care* also encompasses a variety of meanings. As a verb, it means to be concerned, have a preference, show an inclination, and exhibit affection. As a noun, *care* means worry, maintenance, and supervision. Sometimes a word with so many definitions isn't helpful, but in this case Francis fully embodied all of these qualities.

He didn't often use the word *care*, because to use the word is usually to stand outside of its meaning. Think about it. Care is a human capacity, a quality or virtue often requiring action, and not expressed fully in words by those who practice it. When a person says, "I am concerned for someone today," you sort of know that the most important part of concern isn't happening right in front of you. And the person who says, "I care a great deal for my brother," or "I worry about him" is actually saying something about his or her mental or emotional state, rather than something meaningful about the brother who is supposed to be the object of care.

Francis did use the word *care* in the way that Jesus sometimes did in his teaching of the first disciples. In Luke 12:15, for instance, Christ says, "Take care! Be on your guard against all kinds of greed; for one's life does not consist in the abundance of possessions," which Francis quotes in his Rule to preface his remarks about how he and his brothers should never handle money. *Take care* means be careful, which Francis often says, reminding himself and others to slow down and pay attention.

CARING FOR CREATION
IN THE PARTICULAR

You have to slow down if you want to be caring. Francis was careful with human beings, but his practice, of course, went way beyond people. His reputation as the "environmental saint" is well deserved, based upon nearly one hundred stories from his life. But it is also a source of misunderstanding. This is one of those areas where we need to forget what we thought we knew about him if we want to see him clearly.

The most common misconception about Francis is that he loved nature. He's the patron saint of animals, of environmentalists, even of the Cub Scouts. We've all seen his statue in a hundred different flower gardens. There he is, looking on benevolently, sometimes with arms extended out from his sides, encouraging the birds to come and nest upon them. If you are a nature lover, or a bird lover, or a lover of flowers, you may have been drawn to that Francis, and for good reason. There are great stories about him in which he shows remarkable concern for and tends to those creatures and parts of Creation. There's no question that Francis was connected to the physical world in ways that saints who lived before him would have found strange, probably shocking, and maybe even heretical—and ways that make him quite different from most of us, too. Francis crossed lines time and again, including the well-established line separating the human world from the animal one. His life was about breaking down those barriers.

But Francis was not a lover of *nature*. To explain or understand his care and affection for creatures in such general terms is to misunderstand how he was able to do what he did, and why his true charism (divine gift) was and still is so unusual and so desperately needed. One of my favorite insights from Chesterton's little book on St. Francis is that Francis did not love in the abstract.[1] Francis did not love *nature* because he never loved anything or anyone in the abstract. To love nature is akin to loving everyone and everything in the universe, and we know that is impossible for a mere human. Francis's gift of caring was specific, which is what is most unusual about him, more than his being drawn to birds. If we generalize a particular love of this lover who excelled at loving particularly, much is lost.

Similarly, Francis did not in fact love "people." This wouldn't have made much sense to him at all. He loved that person, he loved this person, he showed his love for Clare, for Leo, for Matteo—the person in front of him at that moment.

Francis's loving was particular in the sense that it involved motion and application. It's nearly impossible to imagine him sitting in a chair and reflecting on what love was once like with someone, or pining away for love lost, or showing love in any way that doesn't include feet, hands, arms, action. Francis's connection to the created world was always specific and always present tense.

He was one of those rare people—like Henry David Thoreau, centuries later—who seems to have been able to walk in a forest or a field that he'd walked in hundreds of times before, and to experience it in the present. He could see with fresh eyes each time.

A Personal Connection
with Creatures

When Francis encountered creatures, he'd connect with them as members of the same wide fraternity. When he purchased doves from the village vendors, he looked on those particular birds, saw his sisters, and then set them free from their cages. This beautiful gesture, the early biographers tell us, was one of the first spiritual expressions of the young convert.

He seemed to look into the eyes of creatures and see himself in them. Animals resemble us, of course, and many animals have eyes that are quite like ours. Francis saw the similarities between himself and animals when he met them face-to-face. He stopped and took the time to care for those that most of us carelessly pass by. He never missed the opportunity to understand all sorts of creatures better, from the birds and animals around him to many of the human beings he encountered throughout the day.

Some have suggested that the silence, or lack of language, between animals and humans is an explanation for the bond that sometimes exists between them. And perhaps there is a way of communicating with an animal that is even deeper than how we might communicate with another human being. John Berger writes in "Why Look at Animals?":

> With their parallel lives, animals offer man a companionship which is different from any offered by human exchange. Different because it is a companionship offered to the loneliness of man as a species.[2]

This rings true for many human-animal relationships, and it may help to explain why Francis was drawn to so many creatures. Communion experienced across species is a reminder of how we all have a common source.

But Francis famously did not remain silent with animals he encountered. He often preached to them, taught them, and even scolded them for allowing themselves to be captured. Undeterred by the obvious barriers to communication, Francis began to touch, listen to, and speak to creatures. He seems to have set out to be near them whenever he could, talking and stroking their fur and feathers. Imagine him as a bird-whisperer, and you will come to understand this aspect of his life. Stories abound of Francis helping animals that have been caught in nets, traps, and cages, blessing and freeing them, but only after he mildly scolds them for being so foolish as to be captured. It is as if he wants an animal to be most fully itself, rather than become something quite different at the hands of human beings.

In the countryside outside the towns, Francis loved animals when he cared for them and tried to communicate with them, even when they were aggressive and potentially harmful. He wasn't merely sympathetic. He treated them as if they possessed emotions, and as if their maladies were explicable.

You've probably heard the story of Francis and the wolf of Gubbio. This creature was terrorizing the people of Gubbio who were, in return, attempting to capture or kill it. Francis heard of the trouble and intervened, negotiating between the creature and the town so that Brother Wolf would cease his paranoid marauding, and the townspeople would care for his basic needs. While the legends of this incident can make it seem unreal, there is no reason to doubt that certain people are possessed of a gentleness and understanding of animals that most of us cannot comprehend.

Another representative story from *The Little Flowers* again shows Francis's care for creatures:

One day a boy in Siena caught some turtledoves and carried them, still fluttering about, to the market. St. Francis, who was always compassionate to creatures, and especially to animals and birds, saw these turtledoves and his heart was moved.

"Will you give these birds to me?" he asked the young boy. "They are innocent creatures which the Bible says are pure and faithful souls. Give them to me so that they don't go to anyone who will kill them."

The boy was inspired by God and Francis's words and he agreed. So Francis gathered up the turtledoves and began talking with them in gentle tones.

"My sisters," he said, "why did you allow yourselves to be captured like this? You are innocent. You need nests where you can lay eggs and multiply as your Creator has instructed you."

With this, Francis took the birds to a place where he then made nests for each of them. And the doves settled down into those nests and began to lay eggs in that place, where the friars also lived. Over time, they became so tame with the men that they were almost like chickens that had been raised from chicks by the brothers. They would even come and go when Francis would bless them.

Back at the market, St. Francis had said to that boy, "You will surely serve our Lord Jesus Christ and become a Friar Minor someday." And so it happened that the youth soon entered the Order. The actions of Francis led to life and joy for some turtledoves, but also to the joy of eter-

nal life for the boy who gave them to him. Christ
be praised. Amen.[3]

The story ends beautifully, with the "life and joy" of the
turtledoves considered before that of the boy!

CARING FOR AND
LOVING HUMAN BEINGS

Think of the care-full-ness of Francis in another way: he
wasn't like the pseudomystic who has been practicing
meditation for so long that he seems almost to float above
the ground. Fresh on the heels of exploring the importance
of spirituality in the last chapter, we should note that some
people can become . . . well . . . *too spiritual*. Prayer, meditation, contemplation, or walking alone in "nature" can become ends in themselves. Saying "I love nature" can be an
excuse to stay in your chair and do nothing, just as saying
"I love everyone" is an easy path toward never truly loving
anyone.

Francis eschewed this approach. Instead, he demonstrated a desire and an ability to love the person or creature
in front of him. He never once in his life or letters or writings said that he loved the people of Siena or all the followers
of the Sultan, or that he cared deeply for the members of
a certain parish. That sort of love simply does not matter.
Generalized love and care exist only in the abstract, as ideas;
they have no real meaning—and Francis was always about
creating *meaning*. Words create meaning when they are part
of a life, when they are put to work.

As a young man turned sensitive to the Spirit, Francis
set out to learn how to care. He wasn't born with that genius.
To care intensely, personally, and with individual purpose

is an art form, and any form of art may be learned. His particular conversion included a sensitizing, a gift of the Spirit that changed him from within. He learned to think deeply, but then his thoughts existed for the sake of action, not as ends in themselves. T. S. Eliot once criticized certain poets by noting how they seemed to think, "but they do not feel their thought."[4] This is where Francis excelled: he felt his thoughts, and those thoughts were easily recognized in the poetry of his life.

Francis was one of those rare people in the history of the world who do that most incredibly basic thing that we are asked to do: love. He looked people in the eye and saw God in them. He saw God in the contorted, Picasso-like face of a leper. He was so converted by this ability to love and care in the specific that he was able to follow up the feeling with actions that also were extraordinary. This new gift of the Spirit enabled him to get down on his hands and knees and scrub those lepers' sores not long after he was so frightened of lepers that he fled in the other direction whenever he saw one.

Later on, Francis used the word "care" in his Rule to instruct his friars on how to receive new members to their order. "The brothers should be careful not to meddle much in his personal affairs," he wrote, and then when the new member is selling all of his worldly goods and distributing the money to the poor, "the brothers and the ministers of the brothers should be careful not to interfere in any of this." So Francis also understood that caring for human beings can mean leaving well enough alone and allowing the Spirit to work as the Spirit does, without human interference.

A Quiet Sort of Gentleness

Early on, Francis cared for lepers, in part, out of a sense of guilt for having previously shunned them. That's often where care begins: we respond to an injunction, or our consciences cry out. Something prompts us to do what is right, whereas in the past we've responded in some other way, or we've simply ignored the need. He continued on this path for several years, mostly doing what he knew he was supposed to do, following Christ's teachings as close to the letter as humanly possible. But during the middle years of his converted life, we see Francis taking a greater turn toward the world in the form of gentleness. He practices being gentle—sometimes in seemingly insignificant ways—in order to train himself to care more deeply.

Francis set out to be careful and gentle in every conceivable way. This is when he saves worms in rainstorms. This is when he gathers scraps of paper on the floor because they might contain words of Holy Scripture—upon them. This is when he protects bees in winter and rescues fish from predators. If these small gestures sound silly, consider a far more recent anecdote from the first meeting in the early 1960s between the famous Catholic monk Thomas Merton and the Vietnamese Buddhist monk Thich Nhat Hanh. The middle-aged Merton asked Nhat Hanh what he had learned in his first year in the monastery. Expecting some profound insight of Buddhist philosophy or spirituality, Merton was shocked by the simplicity and practicality of the younger man's response: "To open and close doors quietly."[5]

This is the sort of wisdom that Francis was gathering in his own context: a gentleness that would carry through into other aspects of his life. He developed a reverence for every creature and thing he encountered, figuring that each had a mystery about it that he couldn't possibly know, but that he was to respect. He even regarded his own illnesses and bodily ailments as his brothers and sisters, rather than as something happening to him. A man who opens and closes doors quietly is on his way to mastering the arts of caring, loving, humility, and kindness. And he will feel one with what's around him, rather than seeking to dominate it.

Leonardo Boff put it well when he wrote, "[Francis] demonstrated with his life that, to be a saint, it is necessary to be human. And to be human, it is necessary to be sensitive and gentle."[6] Francis extended his gentleness even beyond animals, fish, and birds; he found ways to connect with, if not "love," animate but unconscious aspects of Creation. This is where Francis's carefulness begins to resemble Buddhist teachings. Thomas of Celano tells us that he would ask his brothers never to cut the whole tree when cutting wood, but only to take off branches so that the tree might regenerate itself. He also instructed the brothers who cared for the community gardens to leave a strip of untouched ground surrounding the plantings of vegetables, where tall grasses and wildflowers would grow and "proclaim the beautiful Father of all. He even orders that within the garden a smaller garden should be set aside for aromatic and flowering herbs so that those who see them may recall the memory of eternal savor."[7]

And Thomas tells us that he spoke with fruits and flowers, spring water and rocks, "as if they enjoyed the gift of reason." Francis walked reverently over rocks, Thomas tells us, adding that he did so in order to show honor to the One who is the Rock.[8] (I can't help but suspect that the carefulness over rocks is accurate, while the theological gloss is all Thomas.) There were surely those who believed he was addled, but perhaps he was conscious of rediscovering something that had been lost through centuries of civilization.

Who else in the Middle Ages thought of such things? His life was full of praising Creation, protecting creatures, and touching the things around him. We have trouble wrapping our minds around all of this even today. No religious school teaches us to walk gingerly, plant flowers, or think about the life of the tree that you are cutting for firewood. And why would a friar imagine that such principles would be of any practical use in life? The finely tuned spirit must understand what the rest of us miss.

An Incarnational Bond with All Creation

It is in this light that we should read another famous anecdote from Francis's life: the story of when Francis created the first nativity scene in a cave near the hill town of Greccio, in the Rieti province of Italy. Every lawn and tabletop crèche that you see at Christmastime today was inspired by Francis's desire to bring that historical event to life again.

Various experiences spurred his imagination. On a recent trip he'd visited Bethlehem, where Christ was born in a humble manger, and he returned wanting people to better appreciate the meaning of the Incarnation. Also, his involvement with animals in every aspect of his life and work was at its peak. The quotidian barnyard noises of pigs and goats and cows were music to Francis's ears. He began to see a deep connection between the humility of God's being born in a stable and the animals that were likely present when it occurred. He understood that salvation was, in a deep and mysterious way, incarnational.

It was mid-December 1223 and Francis had recently returned from Rome, where his Rule had finally been approved by the pope. He was already experiencing some of the pains and discomforts that would lead to his death three years later. As usual, he was on the road, and he selected the town of Greccio for this incarnational experiment.

Francis found a mother who had just given birth, a proud father, and an infant. Beside them he assembled a cow, a donkey, and probably a goat, a chicken, and whatever else he could find to lend the scene a crude authenticity. All the people came out to see, holding candles in the night. A priest began saying the Mass, and Francis preached about the humility of God and the connections between all of us. "The night was lit up like the day, and it was delightful to both humans and animals. . . . When it was over, each one returned with joy to his own place," summarizes Thomas of Celano.[9]

I imagine Francis, in the days leading up to the reenactment of the nativity, seeking out families and visiting farms so as to watch cows calving and goats kidding, his eyes wide with awareness of the messy beauty of it all. A boy or man would never have witnessed his mother or any other woman giving birth in the late Middle Ages. Men would stand outside, banished from the home if necessary by female attendants or midwives. But Francis was fascinated and deeply touched by the intimacies of birth and death. A few centuries before the phrase existed in Italian or the word in English, he appreciated *l'essere terroso*, the "earthiness" of it all.

Not everyone was enamored of such earthiness. Francis lived during the height of the original Gothic era in church architecture, when religious people increasingly believed that the mind should turn away from the coarseness of the world; arches, spires, buttresses, and pinnacles were supposed to point the mind upward, toward the world to come, for that is where the promise of Christian hope was to be found. Gothic art in frescoes, altarpieces, and stained glass highlighted saints and angels, rather than things of this earth.

But Francis found beauty in the ordinary things of the world around him that others thought were prosaic or ugly. In line with this earthy approach to faith, Francis approached the end of his life sensuously and carefully. He lay down on the ground as he was dying because he wanted to feel the dirt on his naked body; this is the act of someone who felt a deep kinship with all Creation. Simply put, Francis was a creature, first and foremost. His was an ancient way of being in the world, showing respect to creatures and things as earlier societies once did, and yet Francis did so from a profoundly Christian, incarnational perspective. He felt a bond with everyone and everything he encountered, imagining that every created thing might be seeking to see God more truly, just as he was. His ability to care for human beings, creatures, plants, and even the inanimate objects around him had taught him a humility the depth of which is difficult to comprehend.

CHAPTER 8

By Embracing Death

*Where we see how Francis embraced
death as an essential and beautiful part of
life and consider that in this area he may
not simply have been ahead of his time,
but ahead of our own.*

Strange as it sounds, death was important to Francis. Not that he looked forward to it—he loved life too much for that—but he recognized death as an important stage of life, and something he wanted to experience.

Imagine the journey of your life, from birth through your formative years as a child, the challenges of adolescence and young adulthood, love, education, friends, disappointments, teachers and mentors, to perhaps more love, finding spiritual meaning or creating a spiritual practice, good work, family, and certain successes, to wherever you find yourself in at this moment. I doubt that Francis ever sketched out his own life of conversion, but I wonder what it would have looked like.

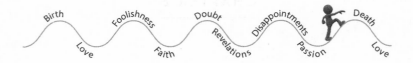

Not every life follows the same course, but this is how I would roughly sketch Francis's journey. To him, eternal life meant life continuous, and death was a stage along life's way, nothing more. It was just another experience that was meant to teach a person something important, as well as usher him on to the next stage in life.

A Time of Quiet Preparation

At the outset, I explained how important it is to recognize that Francis's conversion could not have gotten started if he hadn't been willing to shut his mouth and begin to listen. He was a talkative, playful, fun-loving boy who always had plenty of friends. By the time he became a teenager he was the life of the party, the one you'd always invite. He had money in his pockets. He was good company. He was happy—at least as happy as anyone is truly happy in such circumstances—as long as his friends were surrounding him. He may not have spent a solitary moment before his twentieth birthday.

But no one can appreciate the meaning of death without first learning to be quiet. There is a long tradition within Christianity that a "good death" is one for which the subject has taken time to prepare. This preparation is a quiet, mostly inner work of acceptance, understanding, and assimilation. On the other hand, we have always tended to fear sudden deaths most, not because we die quickly (that actually seems like a *good* thing), but because we might not have gotten ourselves ready.

The genre of spiritual literature known in Latin as *Ars moriendi*, or "The Art of Dying," did not originate until nearly two centuries after Francis's death. Then, inspired by the frightening, nearly apocalyptic sense of dread left by the Black Death that had swept Europe a half century earlier, priests and religious created elaborate manuals for guiding both the healthy and the sick through the end of life. The goal of *Ars moriendi* was to convince Christians that death needn't be feared, especially if you followed a certain protocol of exposing sins in your life, such as pride and lack of faith, and carefully replacing them with virtues, such as thankfulness and trusting in God.

Although such elaborate instruction manuals for the dying didn't exist in Francis's century, the fear of dying unprepared was just as keenly felt. A person's soul must be prepared to meet its Creator, Christians believed then, just as most do now. But we can hardly imagine the terror that filled medieval people's hearts at the idea of expiring without having made some basic preparations. The moments before death were the most important moments of a person's life. One hoped desperately for a "deathbed experience," a time when all of these preparations could adequately be made. The dying would hopefully utter prayers of faithfulness, and a priest would say blessings over him, putting the immortal soul into its best possible position for eternal life in heaven.

At the dreaded opposite end of the spectrum was to suffer death by murder, which was perceived as a sort of double death—one earthly and one eternal—if there was no time for preparing the soul before breathing one's last. This belief is why murder was usually punished so quickly and so brutally in the ancient and medieval eras. This is also why knights and mercenaries, before going off to war, were quick to claim themselves "holy crusaders," since sudden death on the battlefield became Christian martyrdom, a wholly sanctified way to go.

Death of the Old Self

It was after returning home from war, where he'd been injured, embarrassed himself, deserted, or all three at once, that Francis began to go off by himself and discover quiet. He spent long hours of solitude in a cave somewhere near Assisi. We don't know precisely where, but it was probably on the 4,200-foot Mount Subasio, which looks down upon Assisi, or in one of the quarries where Subasio's limestone had been excavated to build the houses of the town. At other times, an unnamed friend would accompany him. And he began visiting churches, including abandoned ones like San Damiano, two miles outside Assisi, to pray. Francis began to love his newfound ability to become quiet with the Lord; and as he was falling deeply in love with God, he was also preparing for a Christian death, almost from the moment his conversion began.

Francis understood that living a Christian life means being ready to die. He was not morose, nor did he spend too much time pondering his end. But from early on in his conversion he desired Christian martyrdom, if that's what God wanted of him, and sought to remove unhealthy attachments.

It has been said—from Sophocles's Oedipus trilogy to Erik Erikson's fifth stage of psychospiritual development—that in order to become a man, every boy must struggle with the image of his father. Sometimes this means fighting with the image that your father has for you, and the result of the fight can be a kind of death of the old self that leads to a new way of life.

His father, Pietro, wanted Francis to be a man like himself: a financially responsible homeowner, respected citizen, husband, and father. Pietro wasn't unlike most fathers today in what he wanted for his son, and he became frustrated when Francis began to turn away from the life he envisioned for him. On at least one occasion, Pietro literally locked his son up in the family basement, waiting for him to "come to his senses." This only gave Francis more time alone, which he'd begun to crave like an addict.

Soon after this incident, we have the famous scene in which Francis meets his father in a public square in Assisi with hundreds of people looking on. Pietro demands that Francis return the valuable goods he took from his shop without permission (even though he sold them to give the proceeds to the poor) and also that Francis apologize. We can imagine the crowd cheering for both sides. *Respect your father! Don't take what is not yours! Listen to your son!* The onlookers must have enjoyed the drama; the scene has a feel that combines Shakespearean tragedy and reality television. The twenty-five-year-old Francis responds by telling Pietro and the gathered crowd that he has only one father, his Father in Heaven, and that he will return everything that is Pietro's to him, stripping the very clothes from his body right there on the spot. An essential piece of the old self's bulwark was jettisoned. In the struggle with his father, here was the definitive death of the old Francis.

The Medieval Fear of Death

So, contemplating death—far beyond simply when and where one's bodily organs cease to function—was a part of conversion itself in Francis's life. He was attuned to what was life-giving and what wasn't, but he was also sensitive to what bodily death means and what it doesn't mean.

Don't let Francis's interest in death confuse you. His was not the macabre fascination that characterized his era. His appreciation for and experience of death are very much part of the radical new spiritual vision that he created for the ages.

The phrase *memento mori*, "remember [your] death," was a near mantra in sermons throughout the medieval period and a big inspiration of what passed then for public art: images of rotting corpses and skulls in paintings and church architecture. Still today, on Ash Wednesday, the priest admonishes the faithful while they kneel and accept a smear of ashes on the forehead in the shape of a cross, "Remember that you are dust, and to dust you shall return" (Gn 3:19).

The Apostle Paul wrote to the Romans in the first century: "Who will rescue me from this body of death? Thanks be to God through Jesus Christ our Lord!" (Rom 7:24–25). I've heard some commentators explain away Paul's words by saying that he was talking not about his individual body but about the deathly powers that rule this world. I'm unconvinced. Paul seems to have been grateful that he would soon leave the world behind, and he had the hope of heaven.

It was upon such biblical foundations that St. Augustine built the doctrine of original sin. Since the first man and woman sinned, the taint of sin has been passed down to every other human being since, and as God said back in Genesis: with sin comes death. "God said, 'You shall not eat of the fruit of the tree that is in the middle of the garden, nor shall you touch it, or you shall die'" (Gn 3:3). So the world itself was seen as full of sin and death—something to be gingerly traversed. There was relatively little about the world seen as "good" in the thirteenth-century Christian worldview.

To journey through life well in the Middle Ages was to realize that evil and demons lurked about. For this reason, the procession and litany of a medieval burial service usually included the rituals of carrying a cross and ringing bells in order "to make the devils flee in terror," as Jacobus de Voragine puts it in his famous book about the saints, *The Golden Legend*. "And so the demons who are in that murky air [are] sore afraid when they hear Christ's trumpets—the bells—and catch sight of his standards—the crosses," he explains.[1] The medieval mind believed that the soul of the departed was struggling to leave the corrupted body, and you never knew how many devils might be assaulting it as it attempted to make its way upward to heaven. Bell ringing was one small way to drive back the devils that waited for their prey like lions in the tall grass.

Numerous theologians, pastors, and spiritual writers over the years have seen it as their calling to write volumes on death, the idea being similar to the words of Ecclesiasticus 7:40, which we still commonly hear on Ash Wednesday: "In all thy works remember thy last end, and thou shalt never sin" (Douay-Rheims). It comes across as very medieval, and for good reason.

Take for instance the twentieth-century Catholic mystic Adrienne von Speyr. A friend and spiritual directee of theologian Hans Urs von Balthasar, von Speyr wrote dozens of books, many of them seeming almost obsessed with death and eternal life. For some Christians in all eras of the Church, this may seem completely normal. Why wouldn't a Christian be preoccupied with death as the doorway to eternal life? Is not eternal life the primary purpose of Jesus's teaching, and of Christianity itself?

This is how von Speyr explains death at the beginning of a book on the subject: "Man lives with one eye on death. . . . He must live with a view to this hour; he must keep it in sight, he must let it have the meaning God has given it right from the very beginning: the meaning of punishment. . . . God banished man from paradise and made him live in a continual awareness of impending death. In God's eyes this situation is for man's good; so man too should accept it as such."[2] With this sort of teaching, she is right in line with the perspective of the late Middle Ages.

In Francis's world, frightful images of death were intended to create fear. *Terror mortis*, they called it, which means "the fear of death" but sounds even worse. We are reminded of the dualistic view of the world that we encountered earlier when discussing the Cathars, who believed that human life was caught between two opposing forces: Good and Evil. The Cathars were dualist in the extreme, but it was a common spiritual and ecclesiastical teaching at the time that life was simply and supremely awful.

In fact, Pope Innocent III, who put down the Cathars, wrote while still a cardinal a popular theological tract entitled *The Wretchedness of the Human Condition*. Here's a representative sample:

> We surely know that human beings were formed out of the earth, conceived in guilt, and born for punishment. All that they do is depraved and illicit, shameful and dishonorable, vain and bad. They are destined to be fuel for eternal fires, food for the worms. They are a mass of rottenness.[3]

A real page-turner, no doubt! You wouldn't think so, but since four times more manuscript copies of *Wretchedness* survive than do copies of Francis of Assisi's "Canticle of the Creatures,"[4] it must be that Innocent III's perspective was more common and more easily accepted than was Francis's.

DEATH LOVED AS A SISTER

Francis seems never to have feared death or encouraged people to fear it. Once again he was way ahead of his time. On this subject, in fact, he may even be ahead of our time.

Francis was no philosopher. He didn't understand death the way the philosophers do when they speak of the immortality of the soul, the prison of this life and body, and the blessedness to come when such things are overcome. The twentieth-century Spanish philosopher Miguel de Unamuno might as well be Plato when he says: "Death is our immortalizer. . . . The sudden and momentary lighting up of obscure matter is a dream; life is a dream. And once the passing brilliance is extinguished, its reflection sinks to the dark depths, and there it remains until a masterful jolt one day rekindles it and lights it up again forever."[5] It's impossible to imagine Francis preaching such words, and not simply because he never spoke of death as an abstract idea.

For the Poverello, life was never imaginary or theoretical, and it was never simply a prelude. Life was the main event of the present, and Francis always lived in the present. He wanted to know and experience and express the love of God right here, right now, each day. In fact, I suspect that Francis was one of those fortunate souls who, had he been informed that his death would come in a year, wouldn't have felt the need to change anything he was already doing over the next twelve months.

It's important at this point to remember that Francis was a singer, a lover of songs. A poet seeks language that is beyond the ordinary in order to communicate something particularly special; to put those poems to song is to aim even higher. Francis had a heart that was part troubadour, part shepherd, and part ascetic. Such a strange combination it was, but it all made sense in his unique life. Francis lived in an age that was still captivated by storytelling and orally transmitted poetry, an age when even the words of Holy Scripture were known almost entirely in how they were pronounced out loud. There were barely any books, let alone quiet, personal reading anywhere outside the thick walls of a cloister.

So Francis sang. He often referred to his body as Brother Ass, for the troubles it gave him. We all feel that way from time to time, wishing that we wouldn't get tired so easily, or could do more. Francis would prod his body along, speaking to it as if it were a stubborn ass.

The Legend of Three Companions, a biographical account of Francis written about twenty years after his death, tells us that, on his deathbed, Francis confessed as sin the way that he'd mistreated the body that God had given him.[6] He realized only then that he'd probably gone too far in forgetting what the body needed as he focused on the work it needed to do. I marvel at the realization itself, as if he knew that he'd hastened Sister Death unnecessarily. Never mind, now he sang to her and of her.

Like a poet who puts pen to paper in order to realize what she needs to say, Francis sang in order to know what was in his own heart, and he sang in order to understand what was happening to him. As you will recall from his "Canticle of the Creatures" quoted in full in chapter four, the final stanza is about death. One might even say that Francis sings *to* death.

The final stanza begins with this famous line:

> Praise to you, O Lord, for our Sister Death.

Sun, Moon, Wind, Water, Fire, and Earth have been addressed as his brothers and sisters, co-creatures of the One God, before Death too becomes a sibling. What simple symbolism, but what power in it! Those who heard Francis compose and sing these words must have done a double take, for never before had death been portrayed as anything other than a source of terror and dread or, in the hands of medieval preachers, a taunt like a stick. But here was Francis welcoming death as an intimate.

MORE THAN HOPE OF HEAVEN

Catholics have always faced death with a certain ambiguity: fear of pain and suffering and possible damnation, mixed with hope of heaven. This is why Francis's whole-hearted welcoming of death is such a radical direction. It is not a conditional embrace. He does not speak elsewhere with extreme confidence of heaven; he wouldn't have been a good Catholic had he done so. *Hope* is still essential to the equation.

No, Francis did not embrace death simply out of confidence of heaven. His understanding of death was deeper than that. If he was welcoming Sister Death so easily and intimately only because he couldn't wait to be ushered into heaven, why then would he have asked his friends to strip him naked and lay his ailing body down on the ground? He wanted to feel Sister Earth, too. He loved her equally.

The medieval attitude toward death in some ways couldn't seem more removed from our attitudes in the twenty-first century. Who worries so much about death in our time? We laugh at death today, not in the way that St. Paul did two thousand years ago with "O death, where is thy sting?" (1 Cor 15:55; KJV), nor in the way that poet John Donne taunted it five hundred years ago with "Death, be not proud, though some have called thee / Mighty and dreadful. . . ." Their scorn was a theological assertion. We laugh at death today because we are able to postpone it so long. Our average life expectancy is more than double what it was in Francis's era. We who tend to have "first world problems" are insulated from most of what killed people back then, especially mysterious disease, malnutrition, and sudden death in war and conflict. And when death is finally upon us, we tidy it up quickly and cleanly, so as to not expose others to its unpleasant realities. How many among us even know what death really looks like?

However, occasionally death's reality hits us in the face—usually when someone close to us dies, or when we are diagnosed with a disease that may be terminal. Then we can become "medieval" ourselves. We wake up in the middle of the night from a dream, sweating, suddenly terrified, imagining what it might mean to actually die.

"Can there be a mystical life without death?" wondered the Catholic poet and writer Raïssa Maritain in her private notebook in 1931.[7] Is it possible to commune with God without believing in the centrality and value of death? On a deeper level, can death be a pathway to a newer and better understanding of God? Francis seems to have affirmed the latter, which is why he welcomed death like a sister; death was essential to life and essential to knowing the God whom he wanted to love in every possible way.

DANCING TO DEATH

There is a sense in the teachings of the earliest Franciscans that religious life—by which they mean what we'd call today "the spiritual life"—is a dangerous thing. To enter into it is to enter into God's living power and expectations. The lazy or insincere person might be better off leaving well enough alone. The third man to become a friar, the distinctive Brother Giles, once put it this way:

> Many people enter religious life and don't put into effect and operation the things that are essential to that holy pursuit. They are like the simple man who arrayed himself in beautiful armor but didn't know how to use it, or how to fight under its enormous weight. It's not every man who can ride a strong horse into battle. And if he would attempt to mount it, he may even be thrown off when the animal rears or runs.[8]

That's a powerful metaphor, and one that Francis would have taught to Giles. Death, like every stage of life for someone passionately involved with religious life, will be intense.

The first text in which we find reference to Francis and his friends as "God's jugglers" comes in what is called the *Second Life*, or second biography, written by Thomas of Celano in 1247. Thomas included in his biography various written accounts of their own memories from some of Francis's best friends—Leo, Rufino, and Angelo—as well as compiled stories from others who were early pilgrims with Francis.

From these sources we learn of Francis's joyful behavior, even when he felt that death was coming. How startling it was to those around him that he sang in the fields and city centers as a troubadour turning his eyes to heaven, and then, at the end of his life, sang also to Sister Death. Francis didn't finish writing and arranging the "Canticle of the Creatures," which celebrates the entire cycle of what God created, until just days before he died.

Francis insisted that he and the friars sing his song, which must have been difficult for his friends as he came to the final verse. They must have known how odd it would sound to those who heard it—just as they would have understood that its sentiment made perfect sense coming from the man they loved. I imagine them singing the beauties of Sister Death while sitting in the courtyard of San Damiano with pan flute, recorder, gemshorn, lute, psaltery, dulcimer, and zither, Francis's face so mangled with the cauterizations and other treatments he'd undergone on his temples, ears, and eyes that he must have barely resembled the beloved friend they knew.

> Praise to you, O Lord, for our Sister Death
>> and the death of the body from whom no one may escape.
>> Woe to those who die in mortal sin:
>> but blessed are they who are found walking by your most
>> holy will, for the second death
>> shall have no power to do them harm.
>
> Praise to you, O my Lord, and all blessing.
>> We give you thanks and serve you with great humility.

Even when he sings that "the death of the body" is something "from whom no one may escape," Francis is praising God. That word, *praise*, appears a total of ten times in the "Canticle," repeating all the way to the end. This is the key to our understanding that for Francis, death is actually something that we are to be grateful for. The moment of death is a blessing, not because life is awful, but because Sister Death is a new kind of gift from God. Hope—our joyful expectation of moving deeper into the divine uncertainty—carries us beyond death.

The only prayer about death that may be more famous than this one is the Kaddish prayer in Judaism. Although it is usually called the "Mourner's Kaddish," it is not really a prayer for mourning but for praising God. At a time when people may be inclined to doubt the reality of God in their lives—when a loved one has just died—praying the Kaddish is a reaffirmation that God is merciful, bountiful, exalted, good, and holy.

As usual with his writings, Francis's prayer avoids theological nuance. The portion of the "Canticle" that is about death is (also as usual with Francis) exactly what it appears to be: praise for the final stage of life. Nothing else. God is good in all that God creates, even death.

But of course the sweetness of the afterlife is part of what Francis is tasting in his last moments and in his song. "For the second death"—the death of the soul—"shall have no power to do them harm." In other words, without fanfare or grandstanding, let the medieval vision of an unpredictable, vengeful God be damned. Francis didn't know that God. He knew the God of love who receives those who love him at death and offers, like a father, to welcome them into the expectancy and great mystery of whatever is next.

PART THREE

WHY FRANCIS MATTERS
RIGHT NOW

CHAPTER 9

LOOKING FOR FRANCIS
TODAY

*Where we come to terms with how dis-
concerting Francis's life was and recognize
him as a guide who can show us how to
allow God into our lives today.*

There were no headlines in thirteenth-century Italy. There
were no newspapers, blogs, or media reports. News traveled by long, circuitous routes, passed on by friends, family,
even one's enemies. News of a battle lost might arrive weeks
later with the return of the few who survived, while word
of the election of a new pope would arrive by messenger,
requiring months to reach from one end of Christendom to
another. Handwritten notes were carried in the pocket of a
tunic or in a satchel over mountains and rivers, for days on
end. The most important news traveled as quickly as a man
could travel on the back of a horse.

Except that early Franciscans never rode horses. Francis
forbade it.

So when Francis died, this important news surely traveled faster than most, but it still took weeks for all the

Franciscans to hear of it, and the friars could not be sure it was true until they heard it from one of their own. Sure, their founder had been ill, and everyone knew how little he seemed to care for Brother Ass, yet no one quite believed he would die. His flying off in a chariot like Elijah almost might have been less surprising.

CHANGES TO THE MOVEMENT

One wonders if Francis's death was hastened by his own sadness. Rigorously faithful to his ideals until his death at the age of forty-six, Francis had watched most of his brothers turn away from them four or five years earlier, and as he lay dying he knew that conflict was already brewing between the friars who wanted to make changes and those who wanted to keep things as they'd been.

The friars who wanted to make changes were deciding that some of the principles in the Rule were too idealistic to be followed to the letter. For instance, not owning *anything*? If you take that principle literally, it's downright impractical; how are friars supposed to survive if they cannot at least begin to own their own houses? Francis wanted them to remain as "strangers and pilgrims" whenever they lived in houses or churches provided for them, not as owners. He wanted them to beg for their daily bread, rather than work to support themselves. This is how he put it in the "Testament" he wrote at the end of his life.[1] But many of his friars couldn't understand this. *Are we really supposed to refuse every gift that a well-meaning benefactor wants to bestow upon us?* they grumbled.

Then there was the idea of avoiding schooling, the priesthood, and positions of leadership—all were teachings

of Francis aimed at safeguarding the humility of the Friars
Minor. Surely a godly man can be a scholar or a bishop or
a cardinal without becoming self-important? But Francis
knew that his movement would not be the same once these
principles began to slip. As one historian has put it:

> His way was to be very different from that of the
> established religious orders and the new Order
> of Dominicans. He believed that God had en-
> trusted him with a very special mission: the lit-
> eral enactment of the Gospel to the glory of God
> and for the edification of others. Until Judgment
> Day should come, he and his brothers were to be
> the animated images of Christ, the quintessential
> actors of the faith, reminding people constantly
> of how the incarnate God had lived in this life
> within the human flesh. A task as significant as
> this could not be compromised in any way.[2]

Among those who believed they could improve on his
intentions were some of Francis's earliest and closest friends.
We can't know their true motivations. Were they making
changes to the Franciscan way because of their love for
Francis, or out of some less noble motivation? We're talking
now about men like Brother Elias, one of the first followers
of Francis, who became vicar general of the Franciscan Order in 1221. Francis referred to him as his vicar and superi-
or, and poignantly wrote in his "Letter to All the Friars" in
1225, "I beg you, Brother Elias . . . by all means possible, to
have the Rule observed without fail by all of us." Immediately after Francis's death the following year, it was Brother
Elias who was responsible for building an ornate, non-pov-
erty-loving basilica in Francis's "honor." This is the beautiful
Basilica of San Francesco that stands today in Assisi. It is

both a magnet for all who are drawn to the spirit of St. Francis and a reminder that his spirit was officially dashed after he died.[3]

Then there was the Portuguese Brother Anthony of Padua, also one of Francis's friends, who deliberately took the order in a scholarly direction. Extraordinarily well-educated, raised in a wealthy home, Brother Anthony began his religious life not as a Franciscan but as an Augustinian Canon Regular. Already a priest and called by the name Fernando, he was inspired to join the Franciscans at the age of twenty-four when he heard of the martyrdom of some of the early friars who'd traveled to Morocco to meet with Muslims. He felt called to the simplicity and humility of the fledgling Franciscans, but once he joined them, his erudition on all matters scriptural and theological couldn't be ignored. He became a famous preacher and interpreter of the Bible and soon began bringing serious theological study to the other friars. Clearly concerned, Francis wrote a brief letter to Brother Anthony in 1224 that included these words: "I am pleased that you are now teaching sacred theology to our brothers providing one thing: as it says in our Rule, please see that you do not squelch the spirit of prayer and devotion in them."

Then there was Pope Gregory IX, one of the most complex and often ignored central figures in early Franciscan history. For many years, he was Francis's close friend and confidant, his only real connection in, and protection from, the ecclesiastical bureaucracy of Rome. He was the cardinal-protector of the Franciscans and often "had Francis's back" during Francis's final decade. It was probably largely due to his close ties to Francis that he was elected pope five months after the Poverello's death. But soon after his election, not only did he call the Papal Inquisition and excommunicate the Holy Roman Emperor for reluctance to

lead the Sixth Crusade, but he seems to have become convinced that the Franciscans wouldn't survive the death of
their charismatic founder unless the order was normalized,
tied more closely to the Roman Curia, and "brought into the
fold," no longer permitted to be so free in its way of being in
the world. He allowed and encouraged the friars who were
making changes before Francis's death to make even more,
and the Franciscans basically became like every other religious order, for good and bad.

The novelist Graham Greene once reflected, "If we had
not been taught how to interpret the story of the Passion,
would we have been able to say from their actions alone
whether it was the jealous Judas or the cowardly Peter who
loved Christ?"[4] So it is as we try to understand the friends of
Francis. Brother Elias, Brother Anthony, and Pope Gregory
IX were complicated people who shared a love and respect
for their friend. Who's to say for sure what the true motivations are for anyone's actions?

But there is no question that, even before Francis died,
institutionalization, corruption, and clericalism began to
sneak in. And when the fun-loving friar who taught his
brothers to live simply was gone, it suddenly seemed that
the fun and the love were gone too, replaced by greater formal connections to Rome, influence, permanent houses,
priestly ordination, and theological training. There would
be very little begging for bread and wandering from place
to place under the post-Francis administrations. The spirit
of his movement exhaled at about the same time he took his
final breath.

A TRUE IMITATOR OF CHRIST

Perhaps you've heard the Italian folktale about the boy
who feeds the crucifix? This story dates back to the Middle Ages and is retold in Italo Calvino's beautiful book, *Italian Folktales.*[5]

A farmer finds an abandoned child in one of his fields
and takes him in. The boy grows up in a rural place, far from
town and church. Reaching adolescence he has still never
heard a Mass, seen a holy picture, or been touched by conse-
crated oil. He's never even seen a crucifix.

One day, his adopted father has business in the city; he
takes the boy along, leaving him in the cathedral for safety,
telling him, "Stay here until I return." The boy quietly and
reverently wanders around, amazed at what he sees. Upon
the high altar, the boy sees a crucifix and, coming closer to
it, notices that a man is stuck upon it, looking uncomfort-
able and lonely. The boy sits down and begins to talk with
the man.

"Are you lonely?" he asks, and receives a nodding "yes"
in return. So the boy remains there, wanting to comfort the
man on the crucifix, asking him what he can do to help.

After a short while, the sacristan attempts to shoo the
boy out of the cathedral at closing time, but the boy replies,
"I couldn't possibly leave this man who is in pain and alone!
I must stay!" The sacristan reports the situation to the pastor, who recognizes a real, even if naïve, form of sanctity.

"Take the boy some food and wine," the pastor tells the
sacristan. And then, you guessed it, the boy shares his food
with Christ, who takes and eats it. The tale ends with the boy
dying at the foot of the crucifix, probably from malnourish-
ment, but being recognized immediately as a saint.

I find similarities between this folktale and the real life
and death of Francis of Assisi. His response to need was sim-

ple and total. His relationship to God was one of devotion bordering on mania. If you read the Gospels and take the teachings of Jesus literally, Francis stands out as one of the only people we can clearly observe in history who was a true follower of Christ. Georges Duby, one of the most prominent French historians of the last generation, recognized this when he wrote, "whatever remains of living Christianity today directly goes back to [Francis]."[6]

But his way of life must have been very disconcerting to the majority of those around him. They respected him as one who did what they believed they could not do.

God Needs Friends

"God has to have friends or else God has no power," theologian Dorothee Soelle once said.[7]

Today, of course, we have a new Francis in the news—the first pope bold or crazy enough to take the name of the Poverello, signaling a desire to reform the Church from the center just as Francis did mostly from the margins. Both by example and by teaching, Pope Francis has begun to return the Church to a Franciscan understanding of friendship, relating to the other, poverty, spirituality, care, and death.

Cardinal Jorge Mario Bergoglio of Argentina, now Pope Francis, seems to be a man whom Francis would appreciate. He smiles. He meets people face-to-face as equals. He touches people who might seem untouchable. He loves to laugh. He is not afraid of change.

We are all watching as Pope Francis is changing things from the underside, leading the Church toward greater humility; revaluing poverty, especially by his own example; and preaching as a last resort to explain the values that he wants to uphold as most important for Catholics and for all people. He shocked the world, for example, when he telephoned a single pregnant woman to offer to baptize her child if the woman's local priest refused to do it; and when he picked up the phone to call Italian journalist Eugenio Scalfari, founder of the newspaper *La Repubblica*, after he heard that the atheist Scalfari had requested an interview. In that interview, Pope Francis said, among other things, that every person should choose to fight evil and live for good no matter what their creed.[8] Even atheists are now saying that being Catholic is cool.

At World Youth Day in Rio de Janeiro Pope Francis went on to say to the millions who were listening: "We want a Church big enough to accommodate all humanity," "I think the Curia's gone a bit downhill," and "I believe this is the time of mercy, a change of epoch." Such statements clearly mark both a dramatic change from the papal messages of the last quarter century and a reclaiming of what is yet unfinished from the Vatican II agenda, but Pope Francis's approach to faith is not without historical precedent. The pope often speaks in the frank, honest language of someone more like Francis of Assisi than a pope, as when he averred in the interview with an Italian Jesuit published in *America* magazine: "I am a sinner. This is the most accurate definition. It is not a figure of speech, a literary genre. I am a sinner."[9]

Some have questioned why Pope Francis didn't simply retain his baptismal name, Jorge, upon becoming pope. Then we would know him as Pope George. In a letter to the editor of *Commonweal*, William Hunt observed, "I wonder what impression a future pope might make upon being elected if he decided not to accept a special regnal name but to retain his baptismal name? . . . The gesture would demonstrate the belief that an identity as a Christian is more important than an identity gained from authority."[10] Perhaps this notion—a really good one—never even occurred to Pope Francis, but perhaps it will to his successor, once Pope Francis has brought more change to the Church.

There is a wondrous spirit in the Catholic Church today, and it is thanks to the Francis of Assisi–style unexpectedness of our new pope. There was the day in late October 2013 when Pope Francis allowed a young boy to play on the Vatican stage while he was trying to give a talk at his regular Wednesday general audience. Pope Francis didn't show a moment's annoyance. He didn't allow any of his assistants to remove the child. Instead, he hugged the boy, talked with him, and eventually encouraged him to sit in his papal chair and listen. The boy did.

Then there was the morning a week later, his general audience just concluded, when Pope Francis met a man in St. Peter's Square who was severely disfigured by neurofibromatosis, a condition that appears very much the way leprosy did in Francis's day. It causes enlarged and sometimes painful tumors and growths all over the body, which makes normal life impossible and human contact rare and unlikely. Pope Francis embraced, blessed, and prayed with the man he met in St. Peter's Square that day, causing the world's press to run to Wikipedia to research how Francis of Assisi had treated lepers, his own era's untouchables.

These are ordinary things; at least they seem ordinary from the outside. I think, in fact, that miracles often appear that way—which brings us to the biggest miracle of all in Francis's legend.

ANCIENT MIRACLES

We have not yet explored the stigmata, the five wounds of Christ's crucifixion reported to have been suffered in Francis's own body in 1224. This is a difficult topic to grapple with, but it is essential to our consideration of what it is about Francis that changed the Church in his day and what it is that can change the Church in our own day for the better. We seek miracles in our lives and in the Church, and God's work manifests itself in the miraculous.

It is easy to simply conclude that the reception of the stigmata is something that occurred in the mystical realm inaccessible to the rest of us, especially to any sort of historical understanding. But this conclusion doesn't account for the importance attached to the stigmata in some of the earliest biographies of Francis. Still, for many people, the stigmata event is the most troubling aspect of Francis's personal story, and there is no escaping it if we want to grapple with both the "real" Francis and his continued importance.

We know that Francis was alone upon Mount La Verna when it happened. Brothers Masseo, Angelo, and Leo were nearby, but he begged them to leave him be for long periods of time. Brother Leo, Francis's closest friend, was bringing to Francis what he needed daily (spare amounts of water, perhaps food) during the time when it is said to have occurred.

Francis was in declining health, and he knew it. He was keeping Lent with his usual seriousness in spiritual practice, fasting and praying. Since his conversion began in 1205, Francis had intensely desired union with Jesus—not just with his mission, but with the person of Christ. And he had a long history of praying before crucifixes.

Francis's was the first instance of the stigmata recorded in history. If ever there were one to believe in, his would be it. All of the others are in some sense derivative of what was said to have happened up on La Verna in September 1224.

However, news of the stigmata did not spread during Francis's lifetime. The world first heard of it when Brother Elias, the vicar of the Franciscan Order, wrote an encyclical letter to all Franciscans everywhere the day after Francis's death. "Never has the world seen such a sign, except on the Son of God," he wrote on October 5, 1226. By 1229 (three years after Francis's death), Thomas of Celano wrote at length in his *First Life* about the stigmata event as if it were history.

Of course there are no firsthand accounts of what happened. Francis kept no journal, and he never wrote about a seraph with outstretched wings flying toward him. No one witnessed or described how that seraph appeared to be nailed upon a cross, and how, after it left Francis, he felt and saw on his own flesh wounds that were just like those suffered by the crucified Christ. For this reason, the most authoritative modern biographer of Francis has recently summarized: "What exactly happened on La Verna on an undetermined day in September 1224? It is difficult to say with any precision."[11] We simply don't have much extant primary material for a good deal of what we "know" about Francis's life.

There were also no witnesses to what occurred between Francis and God in the lonely church of San Damiano, early in his conversion. Francis was alone then, too, but we have less trouble "accepting" the earlier event, even though it also involves something miraculous—God speaking to a human being, telling him to rebuild God's Church.

A renowned biographer of Czech writer Franz Kafka recently explored a similar difficulty—attempting to understand his subject's personal experiences that were never recorded. That biographer posed a question, referring to Kafka, which could just as easily relate to Francis: "What does [a representation of his daily doings] mean for a person whose life unfolds in the depths, in an overwhelmingly inner intensity?"[12] There is more to understanding a personal event than simply knowing what happened when.

The problem with the stigmata story is knowing what to make of it. Is it a scientific miracle—an instance of God altering the course of human events by doing something completely inexplicable on the body of one of his favorites? A couple of hundred years ago, one of the Hasidic rebbes said of the miracles related to the founder of Hasidism, "Whoever believes all of the miracles of the Baal Shem Tov is a fool, but whoever denies them is an unbeliever."[13] There is deep wisdom in that paradox. There are reasons why traditions define certain elements of a saintly life as legends: most of all, because they are not meant to be scientifically defined. That's what makes them mysteries.

Experts have pointed to Brother Elias's possible motives for disclosing the existence of the stigmata as a reason to doubt his testimony. Especially once Elias and others moved the order away from the founder's principle of absolute poverty, an appeal to new miracles would have been opportune. But ultimately, to speculate on such matters is to continue examining a mystical event as if we will ultimately label it "true" or "false." We won't.

I've deliberately left mention of the stigmata until now because the suffering of the wounds doesn't have to be more important than the other aspects of Francis's life. In fact, Francis and his first followers may have found whatever happened to him upon the mountain to be *less* important than many of the other miraculous moments he was privileged to be a part of. Perhaps that is why he never spoke of it. Francis's love for God and others is the true miracle of his life. I would go so far as to suggest that this superhuman love is the miracle in his life that has never been repeated.

I believe that Francis is the last person who would presume to claim a close identification with the Passion of Jesus Christ. Once again, as we've done throughout this book, let us consider not just what Francis said and did, but what he *didn't* say and do. Nowhere do we see Francis claiming to have received wounds that simulated or reproduced the wounds of Christ on his body. He never praised Sacred Wounds like he praised Brother Wind and Sister Moon. Francis after all wrote a small volume's worth of letters, rules, and spiritual instructions. He often reflected in prose, verse, preaching, and song on what we might call romantic experiences—particularly with poverty (Lady Poverty). He occasionally reflected on what we might call dogmatic and liturgical experiences, as when he wrote about the importance of caring for any piece of paper bearing words of Holy Scripture on it. But he never, ever, reflects for others on what we could call otherworldly, mystical experiences.

Francis may not have understood what happened to him on La Verna. Perhaps the stigmata story is an exaggeration of what he experienced. He surely had a profound, beautiful, unitive experience of God. May it someday happen to you and me. But I suggest that Francis would not have wanted a supernatural miracle to overshadow the story of what his converted life was all about. Let's leave it at that. He appeared in death like a man united with his crucified Lord. What else is there for us, with our capacities, to understand?

Most important is the miracle of Francis's life—and how similar miracles can take place today. What matters is Francis's love—almost like a Sufi might express it—for knowing God inside of him. Throughout his life his connection with God and the Creation was stunning, and this is what allowed him to change the world in concrete ways.

MODERN MIRACLES

Miracles happen in the most ordinary ways, and yet they surprise us—because we forget that we make miracles happen. The most common miracle in the world is the one that requires our participation to bring it about. The spiritual and physical power, if you will, is given to us by God, but we are the locomotives.

When Pope Francis challenges clericalism, or parishes renew their commitment to serving the needs of the poor and disadvantaged, it is a miracle. The established order of things has been disrupted. When the pope launches a survey of the faithful to gauge their feelings and opinions, asking every bishop throughout the world to ask the faithful for their opinions about divorce, gay marriage, and contraception, it is nothing short of miraculous. Since when do bishops ask the faithful to weigh in on Church teachings? There are those in the Church who say that these actions evidence a lack of strong leadership. I would say instead that they are the marks of an unpredictable leader like Francis of Assisi. They represent a form of leadership that we haven't seen in a very long time, and one that I hope is able to live on after Pope Francis is gone.

We may not recognize the Church of the future if we use the recent past as our measure and lens. Pope Francis is well aware that the world is watching. In Assisi on the feast day of St. Francis in 2013, while standing in what is called the "stripping room," the symbolic place where we recall how Francis stripped himself of his clothes in order to tell his father that he was leaving behind worldliness, he said:

> My Brother Bishop said that this is the first time
> in 800 years that a Pope has come here. In re-
> cent days the newspapers and media have been

stirring up fantasies. "The Pope is going to strip
the Church, there!" "What will he strip from the
Church?" . . . This is, indeed, a good occasion to
invite the Church to divest herself. But we are all
the Church! All of us! . . . Today she must strip
herself of a very grave danger, which threatens
every person in the Church, everyone: the danger of worldliness. The Christian cannot coexist
with the spirit of the world, with the worldliness
that leads us to vanity, to arrogance, to pride.
And this is an idol, it is not God. It is an idol!
And idolatry is the gravest of sins![14]

This transformed, perhaps unrecognizable, Church that
Pope Francis envisions will be one in which the Spirit of
God is at work.

One of the Hasidic tales of Martin Buber brings out what
I think Francis of Assisi understood, and what we too easily
miss when we look at his life:

One day, when he was receiving learned guests,
Rabbi Mendel of Kozk astounded them by asking
all of a sudden, "Where does God dwell?" They
laughed at him: "What's the matter with you? Isn't
the world full of his glory?" But the rabbi himself
answered his question: "God dwells where he is
allowed to enter."[15]

The miracle isn't that Francis was a medieval man ahead
of his time who understood that human beings are creatures
in the midst of a vast Creation, but that he found ways of inviting God into every aspect of life. The path he began eight
hundred years ago is becoming clear once again.

CHAPTER 10

FRANCIS IN THE FUTURE

Where we see that we have the opportunity to participate in recreating the Church after the spiritual vision of Francis because "the future" doesn't really exist.

Francis of Assisi had no ideas whatsoever about "saving the Church." I am quite sure that no such grandiose notion ever entered his mind. In 1205 when Francis heard God asking him to rebuild his church, Francis understood it to mean literally the church in which he was praying; he started to gather bricks. "Saving the Church" is *my* construct, my observation of what happened next. And I also see that the spirit of that transformation is accessible to us today.

NO BLUEPRINT BUT THE BEATITUDES

Francis was deliberately simple and naturally so. Bright, imaginative, artistic, industrious, and kind, he was adept at responding to the situations he faced with easy, organic solutions. His solutions nearly always involved him personally; when he sent some of his friar-friends away to do something, he had almost always done it first himself.

Francis wasn't an organizer. He didn't strategize or plan. He was thoroughly Spirit-inspired in his approach to life. He had no "ministry" as we understand the term. Life, faith, and work were all of a piece for him. He was simply being himself while doing and saying the things that we now recognize as remarkable. This is probably why one of our best experts on Francis's life, Dominican scholar Augustine Thompson, recently wrote, "Francis was more about being than doing."[1] That statement may seem to contradict what we've witnessed, except that, for Francis, the doing was a natural outgrowth of who he was.

This doesn't mean that a person may become a saint by accident. But there is also a sense in which being truly Spirit-inspired means not having to try so hard. You never get the feeling that Francis was *persevering*. He had doubts but they were mostly about himself. No great feats of willpower were required for what he accomplished. Once he allowed God to enter his life, and his conversion began, Francis was consistently moved by the Spirit that filled him. Thereafter he did what we all could do if we were, like Francis, paying careful attention and remaining faithful to who we are meant to be.

This is where the juggling and clowning comes into view: it was mostly impromptu. At those moments when Francis confounded his contemporaries by doing things that made little strategic sense, they were right to feel confounded. How could he really give no thought to what would happen next week, next year? How was it possible to grow a religious movement without planning for success? Francis never stopped long enough to answer his critics, but he was always listening to God.

Imagine a strategy for growing a religious movement that follows the honest, forthright, somewhat bumbling path of unprepared but earnest, Spirit-attuned people. Most of what Francis and his followers did was follow the teachings of Jesus to the letter. If it looked like clowning around from time to time, don't blame Francis; you should probably put the blame on Christ. The "plan" that Francis and his first friars followed was right there in the Beatitudes, the Sermon on the Mount, and they literally fell into their success—which they didn't intend or desire. If you can imagine their bumbling, unprepared path, you've begun to sense that almost magical time eight hundred years ago.

The secret to understanding Francis and his spiritual vision is that what he did can never be precisely repeated. There is no mission plan or strategy of engagement that could duplicate what the first Franciscans accomplished. If anyone ever proposes to you a five- or seven-point plan for cultivating the spirituality of Francis of Assisi, run the other way. The Spirit inspires everyone differently. We can only make ourselves more ready to do what we are supposed to do.

The principles of Francis's spiritual vision are taken straight out of the Gospels. Those who follow those principles today, I suspect, do it in ways that largely go unnoticed. They are ordinary people who quietly imitate Jesus and live out his teachings in faithful detail. I cannot point you to any living examples. Instead, let me suggest that the moment we hear about their "successes" is probably about the same time that their charism is being spoiled by outside expectations, publicity, image consultants, and building fundraising.

PAST, PRESENT, FUTURE

What does the future hold for Francis of Assisi? The funny thing about the future is that it does not really exist. We know that it doesn't, and yet we talk about it as if it does. That's what's confusing. I'm talking about how we use *future* as a noun. A noun is a person, place, or thing. But which one of those is *future*? If it is a thing, what sort of thing is it? If a place, where do we find it?

"There is no future; there never is any future. What is known as the future is one of the greatest of lies. . . . There is no tomorrow!" exclaimed Miguel de Unamuno.[2] That is how Francis seems to have lived. The future is only, at best, a posture. Social philosopher Eric Hoffer observed that "fear of the future causes us to lean against and cling to the present, while faith in the future renders us receptive to change."[3] This means that with faith we can prepare ourselves to be open and ready for what comes next.

One gets the impression that Francis was always ready for the next change. In the six ways described in this book— and surely there are more—he left behind a vision for life and faith that was markedly, perhaps even dangerously, different from what was usually heard and practiced in the Church of his day. And he was only able to do this, I'm convinced, by listening to his heart and sincerely believing that there was no tomorrow. The future didn't exist for Francis. Otherwise, each moment wouldn't have been so new.

Francis felt a close kinship with Jesus and the first disciples. He reached back into the past, connecting with its reality, as he discovered how to put friendship first, bridge otherness, love being poor, respond spirit to Spirit, care for the creatures he came across, and finally lie down to die. For him, in contrast to the future, the past was very real.

There are vital connections between people of past eras and people today. A deep continuity between the past and the present is at work in all our lives—or it can be. Francis's life was a series of constructions: he built one relationship upon another, using his own friendship with Christ as the foundation.

And, in some mysterious but real way, Francis's life is still both past and present. What happened long ago is still with us, like a subterranean river that runs beneath a grove of fruit trees, feeding its waters into the roots of what grows above. While surface events and developments create unique situations for each new era, like the wind and storms that may batter our treetops, we still live with the past as our roots draw up the essence of what we need to live and grow. It is this nexus of present, Spirit, and past that animates us.

We can't be who Francis was. We aren't, in fact, supposed to be. The secret is to find the nexus, open ourselves to it, and align ourselves with it. Only then will the future begin to make sense—because we give it meaning.

Who knows what the next few years will bring. As a Catholic who is interested in the positive role the Catholic Church can play in sanctifying (literal definition: "making sacred") the world, I'm anxious to be a part of the vision that Francis realized long ago and conscious that we live in a world ready for our making today.

A generation after Francis of Assisi's death, the theologian and "Doctor of the Church" Thomas Aquinas said, "The art of sailing governs the art of shipbuilding."[4] That's just as it should be! It is in that spirit that Pope Francis is calling us to recreate God's Church to better foster the art of true gospel living. If we follow through and don't get waylaid by the sorts of impediments that stymied Franciscanism after one decade, the Catholic Church—and the world—will soon look dramatically different. As we go, we must move forward in the knowledge that the future doesn't really exist.

At the end of his life, in his "Testament," Francis of Assisi wrote:

> This is a remembrance, admonition, exhortation, and my personal testament which I, your little Brother Francis, make for you, my brothers, so that we may all observe the Rule we have promised to God.

All that really exists are people who are listening and responding to God, promising to do simple, seemingly impossible, things.

ACKNOWLEDGMENTS

As I contemplate what has gone into this book, I'm conscious most of all of the face that looks down at me each morning as I write. I'm not referring to a mystical experience or to God, but to the framed photograph of the French Protestant pastor-turned-scholar Paul Sabatier that hangs above my desk. Reading Sabatier's biography of St. Francis in high school quite literally changed my life and created in me a love for the life of the Poverello, as well as a desire to live closer to the teachings of Christ.

I know that I have many living people to thank, too. First, I am grateful to the energetic and efficient publishing team of Tom Grady, Robert Hamma, and company at Ave Maria Press in Notre Dame, Indiana. Having known these good people for twenty years before finding an opportunity to work directly with them on a book project, I am encouraged by their excellence at every turn to believe that the era of good book publishing is far from over!

Thank you to Lil Copan, who caught the vision for this book early on, and who edited it with her usual excellence.

Thank you also to Dr. Mark Bosco, S.J., director of the Hank Center for the Catholic Intellectual Heritage at Loyola University in Chicago, who graciously offered use of a summer office at the Hank Center in 2013. Lunches with Professor Michael Murphy, associate director of the Hank Center, were an added benefit.

Many thanks finally to the good people of Nevei Kodesh, the synagogue in Boulder, Colorado, where I first presented this material to a mostly Jewish audience, and discussed it afterwards with that great interpreter of Hasidic Judaism, Reb Zalman Schachter-Shalomi. This experience convinced me, at a time when I needed it, that Francis's vision is for everyone.

And thank you to my friend Brendan Walsh for asking me in the spring of 2009, as we stood in St. Peter's Square talking about the difference between the Catholic Church today and the spirit of St. Francis, "Why don't you just become a Catholic?"

STUDY GUIDE

PART ONE: A NEW LOOK AT FRANCIS

This opening portion of the book aims both to dispel myths about Francis and to point you in new directions for seeing the "real" Francis amid the legends and misconceptions. It presents a Francis who is quite different from the garden statuary and the myths, neither of which are very useful.

While reading chapter 1, consider these questions:

1. Are you drawn to books about historical figures? Why or why not?
2. Do you come to this book already admiring Francis of Assisi? (Not everyone does.) Why or why not?

While reading chapter 2, consider these questions:

3. Have the famous legends about Francis made you like him, dislike him, or some combination of both?
4. Does the "real" Francis appeal to you more or less than the "statue" Francis?

PART TWO: SIX WAYS FRANCIS QUIETLY
CREATED A SPIRITUAL VISION
FOR THE AGES

This is the core teaching of the book, with each chapter focusing on one important aspect of Francis's life, charism, and message. In some ways, he was ahead of his time; by the final chapter, here, I try to show that he may have been ahead of *our* time.

While reading chapter 3, consider these questions:

5. Friendship isn't a typical place to start when looking at themes in the life of a famous saint. Can you think of any other figure in history for whom friendship might be the first defining characteristic of his/her spirit?

6. Do you see similarities between St. Francis's approach to friendship and Pope Francis's teachings about putting people first? In this chapter, I suggest that Francis became a saint through his gift for friendship. The papacy of Pope Francis suggests that the Pope too feels that personal friendship is our first responsibility. (See "A Good Human Being" on pages 49–50.) In July, 2013 the Pope said, "If someone is gay and he searches for the Lord and has good will, who am I to judge?" Two months later, he was asked how God feels about homosexuality. He replied, "When God looks at a gay person, does he endorse the existence of this person with love, or reject and condemn this person? We must always consider the person." Does this sound like something Francis of Assisi would say, were he living in our age? Why or why not?

While reading chapter 4, consider these questions:

7. In this chapter, I argue that Francis's actions toward people regarded as "other" show that he saw the world differently from most people in his age. Are you convinced? Do you agree?

8. The "Ultimate 'Other'" in medieval Christendom was the Muslim. Pause and consider what Francis did during the Fifth Crusade to meet the Sultan. What might Francis's example say to us today, when once again Christians and Muslims often face each other as enemies?

9. I suggest that we are all limited in our prayer by our image of God (see page 66). What is your primary image of God? How does that image lead you to pray?

While reading chapter 5, consider these questions:

10. In every era, people have looked upon mendicancy as inaccessible to them, given their responsibilities. They have family to care for, children to raise, and work to do. In India, it is generally understood that one is a responsible householder first, and only in retirement may one consider becoming a wandering ascetic or a *sannyasin*. Francis's framework was the teachings of Christ in the gospels; they told him that mendicancy was the condition that all Christians are called to. What do you think?

11. How might revisiting Christ's teachings about poverty change how you look at possessions, security, and your neighbors?

While reading chapter 6, consider these questions:

12. Francis's era wasn't a time when clergy and the Church were very focused on what we today call

spirituality. There were few discussions of how to aid one's spiritual life; what mattered was one's journey in the sacraments, from birth to death, as well as keeping the commandments. That's what it meant to live a life with Christ. Today, the situation is quite different, with many options of what we call spirituality. What do you think of this change? What's good about it? Is there anything perhaps not so good about it?

13. Everyone seems to have a different understanding of spirituality today. Is there any sense in which you find the medieval approach easier and more clarifying?

While reading chapter 7, consider these questions:

14. On page 105, I write that "you have to slow down if you want to be caring." What do you think of that idea? Is that true in your life?

15. Francis always loved and cared in particular, not in general. Try practicing this in your own life in a simple way: On your next walk, instead of admiring a sunset or a forest of trees, examine a particular tree closely and use your other senses (touch) to become acquainted particularly with what you might otherwise just "admire."

16. How might being careful with inanimate objects teach you to be loving and careful with other people?

While reading chapter 8, consider these questions:

17. In the opening sentence, I suggest that "death was important to Francis." Does that sound crazy, or can you identify with this?

18. At the top of page 118, I sketched Francis's life journey from birth to death. Take a few moments to sketch your life journey so far. Where are you on the path?

PART THREE: WHY FRANCIS MATTERS
RIGHT NOW

This short, final part is all about the present and future. We read about the past in order to look forward to the future.

While reading chapter 9, consider these questions:

19. In this chapter, there is a discussion of the stigmata and its role in defining the life of Francis. What do you think about what I say about that event?

20. In the generation after Francis's death, the Christian world witnessed two great theologians: a Dominican named Thomas Aquinas and a Franciscan named Bonaventure. Both became saints and Doctors of the Church, but their approaches were incredibly different. St. Thomas's theological system was built on philosophy, while St. Bonaventure's was built on mysticism. Which approach has played more of a guiding role in the Church over the last 750 years? Which may become the perspective of the future?

21. Is your own vision of God a combination of philosophical and mystical?

While reading chapter 10, consider these questions:

22. Pope Francis is rebuilding the Catholic Church in our own time. Do you see him exhibiting any of the six aspects of what I've described as St. Francis's "spiritual genius"?

23. In November of 2013 the Vatican asked bishops around the world to survey the people in their dioceses about family life. The survey was a step of reform that began with friendship, the first theme from Francis of Assisi's life. The bishops were asked to lis-

ten without talking or interpreting. The *New York Times* reported: "Alberto Melloni, a Vatican historian, said the questionnaire is especially significant because it seeks a snapshot of Catholic families as they are, and uses a nonjudgmental tone to gauge opinions on the church's pastoral response to contentious issues. 'It asks to start with the reality of the family, not the doctrine of the family,' said Mr. Melloni."[1] What else might change if we took seriously the teaching of Thomas Aquinas on page 155: "The art of sailing governs the art of shipbuilding"?

For Further Reading—Please don't skip this. There's good stuff, there!

Pace e Bene, Jon

NOTES

A Brief Chronology

1. Augustine Thompson, O.P., offers the best setting and explanation of this scene that I've seen, in *Francis of Assisi: The Life* (Ithaca: Cornell University Press, 2013), 26–27.

Also, here are those three passages from the NRSV, with the most relevant phrases **in bold**. Francis formed his life and Rule around these teachings of Jesus:

> As he was setting out on a journey, a man ran up and knelt before him, and asked him, "Good Teacher, what must I do to inherit eternal life?" Jesus said to him, "Why do you call me good? No one is good but God alone. You know the commandments: 'You shall not murder; You shall not commit adultery; You shall not steal; You shall not bear false witness; You shall not defraud; Honor your father and mother.'" He said to him, "Teacher, I have kept all these since my youth." Jesus, looking at him, loved him and said, **"You lack one thing; go, sell what you own, and give the money to the poor, and you will have treasure in heaven; then come, follow me"** (Mk 10:17–21). Then Jesus called the twelve together and gave them power and authority over all demons and to cure diseases, and he sent them out to proclaim the kingdom of God and to

heal. He said to them, "**Take nothing for your journey, no staff, nor bag, nor bread, nor money—not even an extra tunic.** Whatever house you enter, stay there, and leave from there. Wherever they do not welcome you, as you are leaving that town shake the dust off your feet as a testimony against them." They departed and went through the villages, bringing the good news and curing diseases everywhere (Lk 9:1–6).

Then Jesus told his disciples, "**If any want to become my followers, let them deny themselves and take up their cross and follow me.** For those who want to save their life will lose it, and those who lose their life for my sake will find it. For what will it profit them if they gain the whole world but forfeit their life? Or what will they give in return for their life? For the Son of Man is to come with his angels in the glory of his Father, and then he will repay everyone for what has been done. Truly I tell you, there are some standing here who will not taste death before they see the Son of Man coming in his kingdom" (Mt 16:24–28).

1. WHY THE PAST MATTERS

1. William Faulkner, *Requiem for a Nun* (New York: Vintage International, 2012), 73.

2. Jacques Le Goff, *Saint Francis of Assisi*, trans. Christine Rhone (New York: Routledge, 2004), 15.

3. Jacob Korg speaking of George Gissing. Quoted in John Halperin, *Gissing: A Life in Books* (New York: Oxford University Press, 1987), vii.

4. Pope Francis, Homily in Sistine Chapel, March 14, 2013 (Vatican City: Libreria Vaticana, 2013), http://www.vatican.va/

holy_father/francesco/homilies/2013/documents/papa-frances-co_20130314_omelia-cardinali_en.html.

5. John Gehring, "Pope Francis: The End of 'Fortress Catholicism'?," *Washington Post*, first published online August 1, 2013.

2. Now, Forget
What You've Been Told

1. G. K. Chesterton, *Heretics* (1905), 60. Many editions are available, including free ones online. Or see *The Collected Works of G. K. Chesterton*, vol. 1, intro. David Dooley (San Francisco: Ignatius Press, 1986).

2. Peter Barnes, *Plays: 2* (London: Methuen Drama, 1996), ix.

3. Most notably, Paul Sabatier in his original 1894 biography, *Life of St. Francis of Assisi*, available today in *The Road to Assisi: The Essential Biography of St. Francis*, ed. Jon M. Sweeney (Brewster, MA: Paraclete Press, 2014); and Raoul Manselli, *Saint Francis of Assisi* (Chicago: Franciscan Herald Press, 1984). Manselli also explains elsewhere why the earliest accounts of Francis, written by his closest friends, are often sad and disturbing: "The important thing was that Francis be seen in all his Christian grandeur and in his human loneliness." See "We Who Were with Him: A Contribution to the Franciscan Question," *Greyfriars Review* 14 (2000): 193.

4. See Dorothee Soelle's posthumously published *The Mystery of Death*, trans. Nancy Lukens-Rumscheidt and Martin Lukens-Rumscheidt (Minneapolis: Fortress Press, 2007), 34–36.

5. Rolandinus Passagerii (ca. 1210–1300), a Bolognese lawyer who wrote a *Summa* in ten chapters on all aspects of law (wills, deeds, contracts, etc.), from which this line comes. Quoted in Jean Leclercq, *Contemplative Life*, trans. Elizabeth Funder (Kalamazoo: Cistercian Publications, 1978), 21.

6. Hans-Erich Keller, "Italian Troubadours," in *A Handbook of the Troubadours*, ed. F. R. P. Akehurst and Judith M. Davis (Berkeley: University of California Press, 1995), 296.

7. Ronald Martinez, "Italy," in *A Handbook of the Troubadours*, ed. Akehurst and Davis, 279.

8. Vatican experts Thomas Reese, S.J., and John Thavis are quoted making points similar to these in an NBC News article, "'Who am I to judge?' The Pope's most powerful phrase of 2013." First published online December 22, 2013 at http://www.nbcnews.com/news/world/who-am-i-judge-popes-most-powerful-phrase-2013-v21984495.

3. THROUGH A HIGH
VIEW OF FRIENDSHIP

1. G. K. Chesterton, *What's Wrong with the World* (1910), 23. Many editions are available, including free ones online. Or see *The Collected Works of G. K. Chesterton*, vol. 4, intro. James V. Schall (San Francisco: Ignatius Press, 1987).

2. *Francis of Assisi in His Own Words: The Essential Writings*, trans. Jon M. Sweeney (Brewster, MA: Paraclete Press, 2013), 103–104. See also Regis J. Armstrong et al., eds., *Francis of Assisi: Early Documents* (New York: New City Press, 1999), 1: 122.

3. Augustine, *Confessions*, trans. Rex Warner (New York: New American Library, 1963), 52.

4. Brother Ugolino, comp., *The Little Flowers of Saint Francis*, arranged chronologically and rendered into contemporary English by Jon M. Sweeney (Brewster, MA: Paraclete Press, 2011), 5.

5. Henri Nouwen, *The Way of the Heart: Connecting with God through Prayer, Wisdom, and Silence* (New York: Ballantine, 2003). This quotation appears in the front matter of the book in

precisely this formation. However, it is actually a summary of three subsections in the chapter on silence; see pp. 42–50.

6. Armstrong et al., *Francis of Assisi: Early Documents*, 1: 194.

7. This is my translation, but you'll find it also in Thomas of Celano's *First Life of St. Francis* in Armstrong et al., *Francis of Assisi: Early Documents*, 1: 194.

8. I am talking, of course, of Nikos Kazantzakis's novel, *Saint Francis* (English 1962), and Franco Zeffirelli's film, *Brother Sun, Sister Moon* (1972). Their combined vision has led many to know a fictional Francis.

9. This is one of the overriding themes in my *The St. Clare Prayer Book: Listening to God's Leading* (Brewster, MA: Paraclete Press, 2007).

10. Thomas of Celano in Armstrong et al., *Francis of Assisi: Early Documents*, 1: 209.

11. *Francis of Assisi in His Own Words*, 85.

12. Ibid., 104.

13. Ibid., 61–62.

4. BY EMBRACING THE OTHER

1. From a letter Henry David Thoreau wrote to a friend in 1848. See *The Portable Thoreau*, ed. Jeffrey S. Cramer (New York: Penguin Books, 2012), 503.

2. From the chapter titled "This Will Kill That," in which Victor Hugo predicts that the invention of the printing press would bring the downfall of churches. *The Hunchback of Notre-Dame*, trans. Catherine Liu (New York: Modern Library, 2002), 166.

3. Guibert of Nogent tells this story in his *Monodies*, which is the first autobiography to appear in the West after St. Augustine's *Confessions*. According to the story retold by Guibert, a Jewish

boy (who later became a monk) was spared when all of his fellow Jews were slaughtered by Christian crusaders stopping in Rouen because the boy was willing to become a Christian and was baptized. Guibert of Nogent, *Monodies* and *On the Relics of Saints*, trans. Joseph McAlhany and Jay Rubenstein (New York: Penguin Books), 97–98.

4. *Francis of Assisi in His Own Words*, 37.

5. André Vauchez, *Francis of Assisi: The Life and Afterlife of a Medieval Saint*, trans. Michael F. Cusato (New Haven: Yale University Press, 2012), 119–20.

6. *Simone Weil: An Anthology*, trans. Sian Miles (New York: Grove Press, 1986), 63.

7. Michael F. Cusato, "Of Snakes and Angels: The Mystical Experience Behind the Stigmatization Narrative," in *The Stigmata of Francis of Assisi: New Studies, New Perspectives*, by Jacques Dalarun, Michael F. Cusato, and Carla Salvati (St. Bonaventure, NY: Franciscan Institute Publications, 2006), 60–61. Francis's "Praises to God" can be found in *Francis of Assisi in His Own Words*, 75.

8. Augustine, *The City of God*, 2 vols., trans. John Healey, ed. R. V. G. Tasker, intro. Ernest Barker (New York: Dutton, 1972), 2: 192. I have modified the translation slightly for readability.

9. Letter from Henry D. Thoreau to Lucy Jackson Brown, July 21, 1841. *The Correspondence of Henry D. Thoreau*, ed. Robert N. Hudspeth, vol. 1, *1834–1848* (Princeton: Princeton University Press, 2013), 77.

10. In his fourth-century apologetic *Praeparatio evangelica*, Eusebius of Caesarea absurdly repeats and affirms the claim of the poet Plutarch that Pan had died. This was absurd because Pan could not exist in Eusebius' Christian monotheistic worldview, but he used Plutarch's claim as evidence that the old pagan superstitions were dead and gone.

11. Martin Buber, *Jewish Mysticism and the Legends of Baalshem* (London: J. M. Dent and Sons, 1931), xxii.

12. *Sensus fidei* is a phrase that comes from *Lumen Gentium*, one of the seminal documents of the Second Vatican Council, and has been recaptured in recent days due to the papacy of Pope Francis. The *sensus fidei* is "the supernatural appreciation of faith on the part of the whole people . . . , aroused and sustained by the Spirit of truth." *Catechism of the Catholic Church*, 2nd ed. (Washington: United States Catholic Conference, 2000), §92–93.

5. THROUGH PERSONAL POVERTY

1. James France, *Separate but Equal: Cistercian Lay Brothers 1120–1350* (Trappist, KY: Cistercian Publications, 2012), xvi.

2. Pope Francis, from a homily he preached at a Mass for catechists on September 29, 2013. Available online at http://www.news.va/en/news/pope-francis-homily-at-mass-for-catechists.

3. "The Assisi Compilation," in Armstrong et al., *Francis of Assisi: Early Documents*, 2: 198–99.

4. Thomas of Celano, *Second Life*, in *St. Francis of Assisi: Writings and Early Biographies; English Omnibus of the Sources for the Life of St. Francis*, 4th ed., ed. Marion A. Habig (Chicago: Franciscan Herald Press, 1983), 481.

5. Brother Ugolino, comp., *The Little Flowers of Saint Francis*, 18.

6. Michel Mollat, *The Poor in the Middle Ages: An Essay in Social History*, trans. Arthur Goldhammer (New Haven: Yale University Press, 1986), 5.

7. "The Assisi Compilation," in *Francis of Assisi: Early Documents*, 2: 151–52.

8. Kenneth Baxter Wolf, *The Poverty of Riches: St. Francis of Assisi Reconsidered* (New York: Oxford University Press, 2003), 4.

6. By Developing
a New Spirituality

1. Archdale A. King, *Eucharistic Reservation in the Western Church* (New York: Sheed and Ward, 1965), 25.

2. *Francis of Assisi in His Own Words*, 97.

3. Ibid., 45.

4. "The First Rule of the Third Order," in *Francis of Assisi in His Own Words*, 43–47.

5. Augustine Thompson, *Francis of Assisi: A New Biography* (Ithaca: Cornell University Press, 2012), 135.

6. Joseph Ratzinger (future Pope Benedict XVI). The quote is from a book published in German in 1970, and it appears in Leonardo Boff, *Francis of Assisi: A Model for Human Liberation*, trans. John W. Diercksmeier (Maryknoll, NY: Orbis Books, 2006), 101.

7. Abraham Joshua Heschel, *God in Search of Man: A Philosophy of Judaism* (New York: Farrar, Straus & Cudahy, 1955), 29.

8. Brett Edward Whalen, *The Medieval Papacy* (New York: Palgrave Macmillan, 2014), 138.

9. Pope Francis, *Evangelii Gaudium* [The Joy of the Gospel] (Vatican City: Libreria Vaticana, 2013), http://www.vatican.va/holy_father/francesco/apost_exhortations/documents/papa-francesco_esortazione-ap_20131124_evangelii-gaudium_en.html#_ftnref20.

10. Robert Penn Warren, *World Enough and Time* (Baton Rouge: Louisiana State University Press, 1999), 3.

7. THROUGH GENTLENESS
AND CARE FOR CREATURES

1. G. K. Chesterton, "The Problem of St. Francis," chap. 1 in *St. Francis of Assisi* (London: Hodder & Stoughton, 1923), particularly pp. 16–17.

2. John Berger, *Selected Essays*, ed. Geoff Dyer (New York: Vintage International, 2003), 261.

3. Brother Ugolino, comp., *The Little Flowers of Saint Francis*, 62–63.

4. T. S. Eliot, writing about Tennyson and Browning in "The Metaphysical Poets," from *Selected Essays* (New York: Harcourt, 1950), 247.

5. This anecdote appears in Michael Mott's *The Seven Mountains of Thomas Merton* (Boston: Houghton Mifflin, 1984), 454.

6. Boff, *Francis of Assisi: A Model for Human Liberation*, 17.

7. Thomas of Celano in Armstrong et al., *Francis of Assisi: Early Documents*, 2: 354.

8. This is my translation, but you'll find it also in Thomas of Celano's *The Remembrance of the Desire of a Soul* (1247), his third book about Francis, in Armstrong et al., *Francis of Assisi: Early Documents*, 2: 354.

9. Ibid., 255–56.

8. BY EMBRACING DEATH

1. William Granger Ryan, ed. and trans., *Jacobus de Voragine: The Golden Legend; Readings on the Saints,* vol. 1 (Princeton: Princeton University Press, 1993), 287.

2. Adrienne von Speyr, *The Mystery of Death*, trans. Graham Harrison (San Francisco: Ignatius Press, 1988), 8–9.

3. This translation is my own. Samples of this twelfth century text are available from various published sources.

4. Brian Moloney, *Francis of Assisi and His "Canticle of Brother Sun" Reassessed* (New York: Palgrave Macmillan, 2013), 106.

5. Miguel de Unamuno, *Our Lord Don Quixote*, trans. Anthony Kerrigan (Princeton: Princeton University Press/Bollingen Series, 1967), xix.

6. "The Legend of Three Companions," in Armstrong et al., *Francis of Assisi: Early Documents*, 2: 76.

7. Raïssa Maritain, quoted in Brenna Moore, *Sacred Dread: Raïssa Maritain, the Allure of Suffering, and the French Catholic Revival (1905–1944)* (South Bend, IN: University of Notre Dame Press, 2013), 1.

8. From *The Sayings of Brother Giles*, my translation. Not yet published.

9. LOOKING FOR FRANCIS TODAY

1. *Francis of Assisi in His Own Words*, 98.

2. Neslihan Senocak, *The Poor and the Perfect: The Rise of Learning in the Franciscan Order, 1209–1310* (Ithaca, NY: Cornell University Press, 2012), 32–33.

3. Then, imagine what Francis would have thought when in 1288 the first Franciscan pope, Nicholas IV, initiated "one of the most ambitious artistic projects of the later Middle Ages, the frescoing of the nave of the Upper Church of San Francesco." Donal Cooper and Janet Robson, *The Making of Assisi: The Pope, the Franciscans and the Painting of the Basilica* (New Haven: Yale University Press, 2013), 1. Once again, what we adore today, Francis would have scorned.

4. Graham Greene, *The End of the Affair* (New York: Bantam Books, 1955), 19–20.

5. Italo Calvino, *Italian Folktales* (New York: Harcourt/Harvest, 1980), 666–68.

6. Georges Duby, translated and quoted in Edith van den Goorbergh and Theodore Zweerman, *Respectfully Yours, Signed and Sealed, Francis of Assisi: Aspects of His Authorship and Focuses on His Spirituality* (St. Bonaventure, NY: Franciscan Institute, 2001), 2.

7. Soelle, *The Mystery of Death*, 45. When she wrote this, Soelle was reflecting on what she'd learned from the writings of Jewish theologian Abraham Joshua Heschel.

8. Pope Francis, "The Pope: How the Church Will Change," interview by Eugenio Scalfari, *La Repubblica*, October 1, 2013. English transcription available at http://www.repubblica.it/cultura/2013/10/01/news/pope_s_conversation_with_scalfari_english-67643118/.

9. As reported in *The (London) Tablet*, August 3, 2013. Each of these statements appeared on the cover of the magazine that week. Then see Pope Francis, "A Big Heart Open to God," interview by Antonio Spadaro, *America* magazine, September 30, 2013.

10. William Hunt, letter to the editor, *Commonweal*, May 14, 2013.

11. Vauchez, *Francis of Assisi: The Life and Afterlife of a Medieval Saint*, 129.

12. Reiner Stach, *Kafka: The Decisive Years*, trans. Shelley Frisch (Princeton: Princeton University Press, 2013), 13.

13. Quoted in Yitzhak Buxbaum, *The Light and Fire of the Baal Shem Tov* (New York: Continuum, 2005), 5.

14. Pope Francis, Address during a Pastoral Visit, Room of Renunciation of the Archbishop's Residence, Assisi, October 4, 2013 (Vatican City: Libreria Vaticana, 2013), http://www.vatican.va/holy_father/francesco/speeches/2013/october/documents/papa-francesco_20131004_poveri-assisi_en.html.

15. Adapted from Martin Buber, *The Way of Man: According to the Teaching of Hasidism* (Chicago: Wilcox & Follett, 1951), 45–6.

10. FRANCIS IN THE FUTURE

1. Thompson, *Francis of Assisi: A New Biography*, x.

2. Unamuno, *Our Lord Don Quixote*, 11.

3. Eric Hoffer, *The True Believer: Thoughts on the Nature of Mass Movements* (New York: Harper & Row, 1951), 19.

4. Thomas Aquinas, from *Summa contra Gentiles*. See *St. Thomas Aquinas Philosophical Texts*, trans. Thomas Gilby (New York: Oxford University Press, 1951), 65.

STUDY GUIDE

1. Jim Yardley, "With Survey, Vatican Seeks Laity Comment on Family Issues," *New York Times*, November 8, 2013, http://www.nytimes.com/2013/11/09/world/europe/with-survey-vatican-seeks-laity-comment-on-family-issues.html?_r=0.

For Further Reading

"Ideas work on minds. . . . An idea is just a staging post to action."

—Simon Blackburn
Plato's Republic: A Biography

"We try to understand ourselves and our world only in order that we may learn how to live."

—R. G. Collingwood
Speculum Mentis, or The Map of Knowledge

Great Modern Biographies of Francis

Green, Julien. *God's Fool: The Life and Times of Francis of Assisi.* Translated by Peter Heinegg. New York: Harper & Row, 1987.

Manselli, Raoul. *Saint Francis of Assisi.* Chicago: Franciscan Herald Press, 1984.

Sabatier, Paul. *The Road to Assisi: The Essential Biography of Saint Francis*. Edited by Jon M. Sweeney. Brewster, MA: Paraclete Press, 2003, rev. ed. 2014.

Thompson, Augustine. *Francis of Assisi: The Life*. Ithaca, NY: Cornell University Press, 2012. A slightly abbreviated paperback edition was published in 2013.

Vauchez, André. *Francis of Assisi: The Life and Afterlife of a Medieval Saint*. Translated by Michael F. Cusato. New Haven: Yale University Press, 2012.

HISTORICAL BACKGROUND AND TEXTUAL CRITICISM

Akehurst, F. R. P. and Judith M. Davis, eds. *A Handbook of the Troubadours*. Berkeley: University of California Press, 1995.

Armstrong, Regis J., J. A. Wayne Hellmann, and William J. Short, eds. *Francis of Assisi: Early Documents*. Vol. 1, *The Saint*. New York: New City Press, 1999.

———. *Francis of Assisi: Early Documents*. Vol. 2, *The Founder*. New York: New City Press, 2000.

———. *Francis of Assisi: Early Documents*. Vol. 3, *The Prophet*. New York: New City Press, 2002.

Brooke, Rosalind B. *The Coming of the Friars*. London: George Allen & Unwin, 1975.

———. *The Image of Saint Francis: Responses to Sainthood in the Thirteenth Century*. Cambridge: Cambridge University Press, 2006.

Dalarun, Jacques. *The Misadventure of Francis of Assisi: Toward a Historical Use of the Franciscan Legends*. Translated by Edward Hagman. St. Bonaventure, NY: Franciscan Institute Publications, 2002.

Dalarun, Jacques, Michael F. Cusato, and Carla Salvati. *The Stigmata of Francis of Assisi: New Studies, New Perspectives*. St. Bonaventure, NY: Franciscan Institute Publications, 2006.

Habig, Marion. A., ed. *St. Francis of Assisi: Writings and Early Biographies; English Omnibus of the Sources for the Life of St. Francis.* 4th ed. Chicago: Franciscan Herald Press, 1983.

Le Goff, Jacques. *Saint Francis of Assisi.* Translated by Christine Rhone. New York: Routledge, 2004.

Moloney, Brian. *Francis of Assisi and His "Canticle of Brother Sun" Reassessed.* New York: Palgrave Macmillan, 2013.

Moorman, John R. H. *The Sources for the Life of S. Francis of Assisi.* Manchester, UK: Manchester University Press, 1940.

Music, David W. *Hymnology: A Collection of Source Readings.* Lanham, MD: Scarecrow/Rowman & Littlefield, 1996.

Thompson, Augustine. *Revival Preachers and Politics in Thirteenth Century Italy: The Great Devotion of 1233.* Eugene, OR: Wipf & Stock, 2010.

van den Goorbergh, Edith and Theodore Zweerman. *Respectfully Yours, Signed and Sealed, Francis of Assisi: Aspects of His Authorship and Focuses on His Spirituality.* St. Bonaventure, NY: Franciscan Institute, 2001.

FRANCIS AND ANIMALS

Brother Ugolino, comp. *The Little Flowers of Saint Francis.* Introduced, annotated, arranged chronologically, and rendered into contemporary English by Jon M. Sweeney. Brewster, MA: Paraclete Press, 2011.

Regis J. Armstrong et al., eds. "The Assisi Compilation," in *Francis of Assisi: Early Documents.* Vol. 2, *The Founder.* New York: New City Press, 2000.

Francis and the Church

Boff, Leonardo. *Saint Francis of Assisi: A Model for Human Liberation.* Translated by John W. Diercksmeier. Maryknoll, NY: Orbis Books, 2006.

Whalen, Brett Edward. *The Medieval Papacy.* New York: Palgrave Macmillan, 2014.

Francis, the Crusades, and Islam

Guibert of Nogent. *Monodies and On the Relics of Saints: The Autobiography and a Manifesto of a French Monk from the Time of the Crusades.* Translated by Joseph McAlhany and Jay Rubenstein. New York: Penguin Books, 2011.

Moses, Paul. *The Saint and the Sultan: The Crusades, Islam, and Francis of Assisi's Mission of Peace.* New York: Doubleday Religion, 2009.

Parrinder, Geoffrey. *Jesus in the Qur'an.* New York: Oxford University Press, 1977.

Francis and Pope Francis

Craughwell, Thomas J. *Pope Francis: The Pope from the End of the Earth.* Saint Benedict Press, 2013.

Pope Francis. "A Big Heart Open to God: The Exclusive Interview with Pope Francis." By Antonio Spadaro. *America* magazine, September 30, 2013, http://www.americamagazine.org/pope-interview.

———. Address during a Pastoral Visit. Room of Renunciation of the Archbishop's Residence, Assisi, October 4, 2013. Vatican City: Libreria Vaticana, 2013, http://www.vatican.va/holy_father/francesco/speeches/2013/october/documents/papa-francesco_20131004_poveri-assisi_en.html.

————. *Evangelii Gaudium* [The Joy of the Gospel]. Vatican City: Libreria Vaticana, 2013, http://www.vatican.va/holy_father/francesco/apost_ exhortations/documents/papa-francesco_esortazione-ap_20131124_ evangelii-gaudium_en.html#_ftnref20

————. "The Pope: How the Church Will Change." Interview by Eugenio Scalfari. *La Repubblica*, October 1, 2013, http://www.repubblica. it/cultura/2013/10/01/news/pope_s_conversation_with_scalfari_english-67643118/.

Wall Street Journal (staff). *Pope Francis: From the End of the Earth to Rome.* New York: HarperCollins, 2013. Kindle e-book.

FRANCIS AND POVERTY

Agamben, Giorgio. *The Highest Poverty: Monastic Rules and Form-of-Life.* Translated by Adam Kotsko. Stanford: Stanford University Press, 2013.

Senocak, Neslihan. *The Poor and the Perfect: The Rise of Learning in the Franciscan Order, 1209–1310.* Ithaca, NY: Cornell University Press, 2012.

Wolf, Kenneth Baxter. *The Poverty of Riches: St. Francis of Assisi Reconsidered.* New York: Oxford University Press, 2003.

FRANCIS AND SPIRITUALITY

Cunningham, Lawrence S. *Francis of Assisi: Performing the Gospel Life.* Grand Rapids: Eerdmans, 2004.

Sweeney, Jon M. *The St. Francis Prayer Book: A Guide to Deepen Your Spiritual Life.* Brewster, MA: Paraclete Press, 2004.

————. *The St. Clare Prayer Book: Listening for God's Leading.* Brewster, MA: Paraclete Press, 2007.

Unamuno, Miguel de. *Our Lord Don Quixote.* Princeton: Princeton University Press/Bollingen Series, 1967.

Jon M. Sweeney is an independent scholar and one of religion's most respected writers. His work has been hailed by everyone from PBS and James Martin, S.J., to Fox News and Dan Savage. He's been interviewed on *CBS Saturday Morning*, Fox News, CBS-TV Chicago, *Religion and Ethics Newsweekly*, and on the popular nightly program, *Chicago Tonight*. Several of his books have become History Book Club, Book-of-the-Month Club, Crossings Book Club, and Quality Paperback Book Club selections. His 2012 popular history, *The Pope Who Quit*, was published by Image/Random House and optioned by HBO. It has sold more than 35,000 copies in the trade edition, was a selection of History Book Club, received a starred review in *Booklist*, and was excerpted by Reader's Digest for their iPad subscribers. He is also the coauthor with Phyllis Tickle of *The Age of the Spirit*, from Baker Books. Sweeney is the editorial director at Franciscan Media. He formerly served as editor in chief and publisher of Paraclete Press. He is married, the father of three, and lives in Vermont